Bringing Bodypainting to Life

A Guide to the World of Bodypainting

by Karala Barendregt

Printed in Austria by: Kreiner Druck 2008

Publisher: info@wbpa.info
World Body Painting Association   www.wbpa.info
World Bodypainting Festival   www.bodypainting-festival.com
Karala B   www.karala-b.com

The author

Karala Barendregt from Sydney, Australia, comes from an arts back-
ground that includes visual and performance arts. She studied dance at
Sydney Dance Development, performed with various drama and vocal
ensembles and studied guitar and song writing with Don Hopkins, an
award winning Australian blues artist.
Since 2004 Karala has been part of the organisational team of the World
Body- painting Festival in Seeboden, Austria, alongside husband Alex
Barendregt who is the creator of the event. She is presenter of the onsite
Festival TV, festival writer, part of the festival academy organisation and
artist contact person.
Karala also represents the World Body Painting Association and spends
much of her year doing voluntary work to support the association and its
members. This includes artist relations, representation of the association
at conventions and administration.
In 1999 Karala first came into contact with the art of Bodypainting when
working as production assistant on a documentary about the art form
with artists Sahra Bull and Darren Marshall from Sydney.
Her main area of studies has been in visual arts focusing on art history
and painting on canvas, an area she continues to explore today.

Thank You

I would like to warmly thank the artists who dedicate their time and
creativity to the art of bodypainting. The photographers who capture the
images and give the art work longer life. The models who put the passion
into the paint.

I would like to thank Sebastian Langer from KRYOLAN for his belief and
support. Mathias Walder for layout. My editor Amalina Wallace for proof
reading. My husband Alex Barendregt for being a balancing and inspiring
second half. Sam Barendregt for making me take the time to finally write
this book.

Content

Iconic artists of our time

Imagine a painter who can create an image
from an idea in the fullness of colour,
design and expression,
and then imagine this artist
asking their canvas to sing, dance or scream.

The art of bodypainting is exploding all around the globe.
An art form where ballet meets Monet.
Where drama meets Dali.
Bodypainting is a modern art form
springing from ancient roots
that brings together painters, performers,
photographers and creative people
from every walk of life.

Karala Barendregt

Why use a living canvas?

Art is a form of discovery, a tool for exploration and a medium of expression. It is part of our human make up to question the world around us and to want to celebrate its beauty. No matter what your personal intention is in being an artist, whether it is social critique, personal exploration or a pure celebration of your part in our world, you will at some point have to choose the mediums you use to create with.

Painting onto bodies is booming in the time we are living but it is no new idea. Traditional cultures have used body art for thousands of years as a way to enhance the rituals honouring the stages of life and death.

The paintings we see today have moved into new directions and a body-painting artist working at the beginning of the 21st century is a painter, a conceptualist, a choreographer, a director and a photographer.

Bodypainting has many uses in many different areas of work, all of them having potential to bring an artist creative freedom and satisfaction. A visual artist may move into bodypainting to give their art a life of its own. A performer may take up bodypainting to create an illusion around their character that is not possible with just make-up and costume. Fashion can be heightened when make-up moves into bodypaint and the film industry can never have enough special effects in living colour.

When you decide to take your design away from a square canvas and wrap it around a living human being, you are adding the endless dimension of human movement, emotion and character to the possibilities of your concept.

Over the following pages we will have a look at what it takes to bring an idea of colour and make it a living breathing dancing work of art. We'll examine the development of this industry and the inspiring artists from all around the world who have taken bodypainting to where it is today.

Art Colour Ballet   Manfred Halbweiss

Bodypainting in Traditional Cultures

Bodypainting has been used for tens of thousands of years in traditional cultures all over the world. Some of those cultures are still practising their traditions today, some we know about only through the records of history and the paintings on cave walls.

Traditional cultures using bodyart demonstrate common links between history, spirituality and the body. Ceremonies are used in every culture to commemorate birth, death, weddings and coming of age. Covering the body with symbols and imagery increases the potency of ritual by clothing the skin in thoughts and emotions. Painting onto the body is a process of transformation and enlargement of the soul.

Bodypainting also has the practical purpose of healing as some natural ochres have antiseptic qualities and can also protect an unclothed body against insects in hotter climates.

The bodypainting from traditional cultures is the root of bodypainting today. It is natural to be inspired by images of traditional bodyart but it is also important to treat traditional cultures with respect and understanding. Many aspects of body decoration are considered holy or private so handle with care. Using images from traditional cultures in your work without permission can be seen by a traditional artist as cultural appropriation.

The following are examples of body decoration using paint, ochre and dye. Tattoo is not included.

The Celts.

Celtic groups adorned themselves with both permanent tattoos and a temporary blue skin stain made from fermented woad. Women and girls stained themselves with blue for their religious rituals, and men woaded for conflict and conquest, using patterns reflecting their rank or affiliation.

Romans and other historians wrote accounts of Celts with blue body art through the period of Roman occupation, but the practice seems to have ended with conversion to Christianity.

Eyewitness descriptions of the patterns describe them as representing animals, serpents and dragons. Intertwining serpents and animals were prominent elements in other Celtic art from pre-Roman times through to the Medieval Period. Woad and indigo will stain skin when they are in the "vat" stage of dye.

For more information read "Finding Blue" by Catherine Cartwright-Jones.
www.tapdancinglizard.com
and visit www.indigopage.com

China.

The 'Peking Opera' of China was formalised in the late 18th century. This is a form of theatre where the players have boldly painted faces to identify characters. Strong lines with intense colours fade into each other covering the face, neck and hands, and combined with bright and lavish costumes create a finished performer who needs little stage decoration to compliment them.

The mask-like face paintings used in traditional Chinese storytelling and local theatre may date back to as much as three thousand years BC.

Japan.

In Japan the geisha culture developed ornate face, neck and bodypaint-ing. Typically the face and neck were painted white to enhance beauty. A large double V of skin was left blank on the back of the neck showing the natural skin in an exaggerated hairline and was considered highly erotic. Geisha lips are overly small, rose bud shaped, while the face may be shaped with varying extremities of red rouge around the nose, check boes and hair line. Eyes are then lined with black on the over lid while hands and ankles are also painted to a pale white.

Also well known from Japan is Kabuki face and mask paint. These are bold mask-like paintings used to identify characters for historical performance and plays.

The Americas.

There are many Indigenous Americans who still use body paint. From simple black lines across the cheeks to mixtures of blacks and reds covering the whole body, these paintings vary drastically. Body painting is used for tribal identification with members of each tribe having common aspects in their body decoration.

Within a tribe the body art can again vary depending on rank and gender. Through the level and type of painting a chief can be recognised from a healer, warrior or carer. This is where body art combines aspects of art and expression with social classification. Patterns and colours may again change for times of battle. Unfortunately much of the tribal body coding has been lost over the centuries but those left today are rich and beautiful.

In South America some tribes also combine body paint with elaborate body and face piercing to enhance beauty.

India.

In India body art has been used extensively throughout the country. Henna painting is the most recognised body art from India with natural pigments being used to decorate the faces, hands and feet of brides before marriage. These patterns can take hours or even days to apply to accentuate beauty.

Paintings on the face and body can also be used to identify people from different castes or social levels. A mark on the forehead between the eyes can immediately tell a fellow Indian what religion, social level or marital status someone has.

Some people cover their whole bodies in paint to identify themselves as someone who has given up day to day life to follow a spiritual path. They are treated with great respect and some apprehension.

Indigenous Australians.

As in many traditional cultures the body art of the Indigenous Australians has deep spiritual significance. Some body paintings are used for story telling, as an important part of passing on history. A person may paint themselves to represent an animal or person from a 'dream time' story, explaining how the earth came into creation and why it is the way it is today. Body art is also used for social order with varying markings being used for gender, social level and role within a tribe.

Designs and colours change throughout the continent. Colours are typically white, yellows, black, browns and ochre. Designs can vary from a single colour smeared across the body to ornate patterns and designs.

Africa.

Body art throughout Africa has many purposes and expressions. In some countries African women decorate and paint themselves elaborately as a mark of beauty. In other countries it is the man who will paint himself to heighten his beauty. These paintings can be combined with piercing and body scarring to form complicated patterns all over the body.

Body painting is also used for tribal identification and to distinguish between important roles within a tribe. A medicine man for a tribe may have
more decoration and be intimidating in his strangeness.

The colours used are made of natural pigments found in the earth but
can still have strong and bold effects in design and application.

Exercises

Choose a bodypainting technique from a traditional culture and study the
meaning behind the symbols and designs. Create a bodypainting using
these traditional colours and with your own symbols, interpret a modern
day ritual from your life.

Choose a ritual or ceremony from your culture and give it a modern interpretation through bodypainting.

Andamanese Bodypaining www.andaman.org

Ariadne Van Zandbergen

Catherine Cartwright-Jones

Erika Harrison   Scott Watt

Modern Geisha   Karen Yiu   Ike

Pop Cult

The beginning of the present day bodypainting movement can be traced back to the 1960s. A cultural revolution swept over many continents and this was reflected in the art of the time. Attitudes to the unclothed body shifted.

Artists experimented with painting onto bodies and pressing the living form onto canvas. The flower power generation appropriated aspects of traditional cultures including body decoration. In the 70s and the beginning of the 80s the glam rock movement took makeup art to a new extreme of expression. The message of the time was exploration. Role playing and expression became not only acceptable but encouraged.

The first modern artist to take bodypainting from its traditional purpose and use it as a modern art was Veruschka. Born Vera von Lehndorff, Veruschka began her career as a fashion model and quickly made a name for herself as a cultural icon.

She was inspired by the ability it gave her to take on roles and explore character. Fashion soon became restrictive for her and she left the fashion world to discover a new realm of exploration that has inspired bodypainting artists for decades since.

Veruschka painted herself as a way to camouflage or change herself. As an animal, a wild beast, a vamp or even blending herself into landscape to completely disappear, her paintings were an innovation in role play. Her work covers a full spectrum from elegance and glam beauty, through gender reversal and into worlds of the unreal. Any artist looking to work with bodypainting should take a deep breath and walk through her images for a moment before picking up a brush.

Exercise
Create a full body artwork to the theme of the 60s or 70s. Flower power, glam rock, music and love!

Brian Dunning   Studio121

Paul Mauriat   record cover

Gerda Fantina   Hans Spirek

Bodypainting Today

Bodypainting is booming all across the globe. Bodypainting, like dance, uses the body to express ideas, moods and stories. Today the industry is populated by many talented and creative people of integrity who are recognised for their brilliance.

In many countries bodypainting is taught in makeup schools. Some people choose to take private classes from recognised artists and some again learn through workshops available at festivals and competitions.

The "World Bodypainting Festival" with the "World Bodypainting Awards" has been a driving force behind the bodypainting movement for over a decade. From its humble beginnings in 1998 the festival has made a place in Seeboden, southern Austria, for bodypainters to meet, to build a community and share ideas. Through its international reach the festival has brought together artists who may not have otherwise met, has inspired new artists to take up the art form and has brought a quality of work into the public eye that has created understanding and appreciation of bodypainting.

The 'World Bodypainting Awards' continue to recognise those artists who have reached the top of their fields and to push for new ideas and innovation. To foster growth in the form, the festival includes the "WBF Academy" which runs workshops and classes in every imaginable area of bodypainting.

Very few bodypainters support themselves by bodypainting alone. Some work as makeup artists, some as airbrush artists and some in special effects for film and theatre. There are also many who combine their work as facepainters and entertainers. The challenge is to find the balance between being able to create and being able to live.

Bodypainting is made up of very different techniques including brush and sponge, airbrushing, special effects and UV effects. These can be combined depending on the result desired.

The purpose of the bodypainting can play a part in deciding which style or techniques to use. Is it an advertising shoot with six hours time to paint or two? Is it in public? Is it for a live show where performers will dance or be in contact with each other? Competitions will have specific rules relating to techniques. Bodypainting in combination with fashion serves yet another purpose. How long does the bodypainting have to last and in what conditions?

Every continent has its iconic artists working in different fields. There are thousands of works that have been created and then washed away. This is just the beginning. There is no end to the possibilities of imagination and the need to create.

Uliana Makhtyuk   Ursula Eisl

Process

The first step to designing a bodypainting is to understand the canvas. The human body is not a flat square. Have a look at some basic anatomical images. Develop an understanding of the way a skeleton is structured. Look at where the muscles are attached to the skeleton and how they move. Look at where fat is deposited on the male or female body. When looking at your model, first think about what is creating the shapes beneath the skin. Look at where skin is being pushed by bone, where it stretches over muscle and where it softly covers fat. Now you have an understanding of how your artwork will move.

Choose a paint that is approved for use on the human body.

Use a picture of the back and front of a man or woman to design your bodypainting. Use the images provided, or, if you know the model you will be using, draw a sketch of them front and back to get the proportions of your canvas right. You can also take a photo of them and trace it if you want to have their exact proportions.

Before you begin your composition, think about the purpose of your finished work. Is it for a private art project, for fashion, for advertising or for competition? See the section 'uses of bodypainting' for further tips.

Draw your design before you begin painting. Have a clear idea of what your finished work should tell the viewer. You may need to incorporate words, images or logos into the design. You may want to have a pattern or design moving over the whole body and let the natural forms of the body create the finished picture.

Whatever your design is, it should complement the shapes of the body. If you take a picture of a face and stick it in the centre of the chest, then paint the rest of the body one colour, you may as well have put the painting onto a square canvas.

Think about how your composition will change when the model moves. It should work as one continuous artwork when the model moves, lifts their arms, dances and stands side on.

Think about the distance of your audience. A bodypainting that will only be viewed on a stage from a distance needs to have a bolder design that stands out from afar. A bodypainting that will be viewed from close up or photographed can have more fine detail.

The face is very important in your composition. The face is still the first place the viewer will make contact with your artwork. Your painting should not hide the expression of the model. Complement the shapes of the face and highlight the features. It can be beautiful or terrible depending on your artwork but it should always make an impact.

Choose colours that will harmonise or contrast effectively over the whole body. You may choose to use only three colours that contrast boldly to create a striking pattern that is effective from a distance. If you are painting with fine detail and lots of images then it is good to use a wider range of colours. Be careful that the colours work well together.

If you are working with brush and sponge technique, experiment with mixing your colours together or with white or black to get variety. Paints in cake form can be mixed directly in the container; liquid paints can be mixed in a cup. Airbrush artists still mix colours but do this directly on the body while wet or by applying very thin layers.

If you are using an image in your artwork then practice drawing it freehand. If you are using stencils then have them cut out before you begin your work and be sure they are the right size for your model.

When finishing painting have a last look over the model and make sure the work is fully complete. Check feet, underwear, appropriate shoes, hair style, hair lines, makeup, and joints such as underarms and behind the knees. Look for skin that should be covered and places that may have rubbed off.

It is a good idea for an artist to buy a collection of G-strings, white, decoration free and in different sizes for a man or a woman. The wrong underwear can spoil a bodypainting. It can also help to have a collection of nipple covers, deodorant, tissues, wet-wipes, hair brushes, hair spray, hair pins, cotton wipes, a mirror, basic makeup, soap, shampoo and to be thoughtful, a towel. If you are using glue then find out if it has a specific remover. Baby oil is good for hard to remove paint or glue. Be aware of your model's needs before, during and after the bodypainting job. Happy models work better. Have a collection of music you can listen to while painting or for your model to perform to if necessary.

Whatever the purpose of your bodypainting the finished artwork should always express a concept, be a complete work and enhance the living model's character. Every bodypainting can be a rewarding experience for artist, model, photographer and audience.

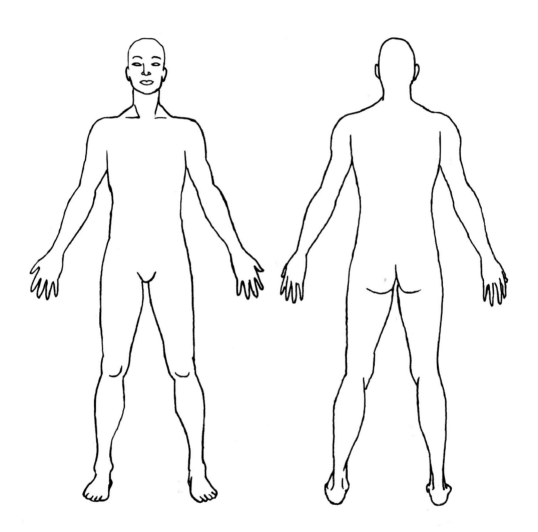

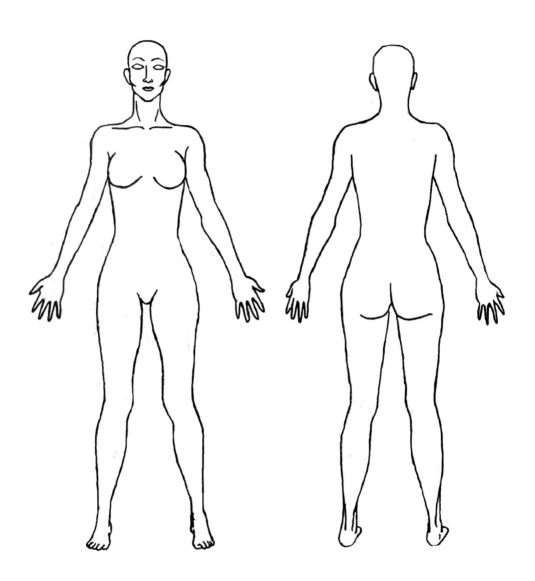

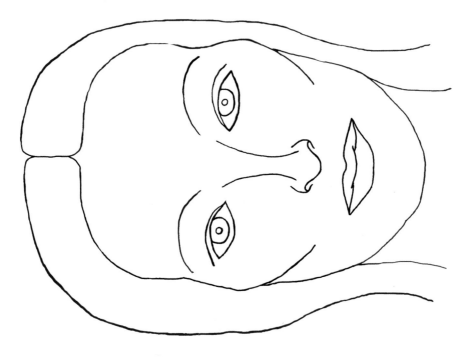

"STEP UP"- A STAIR OF YOUR LIFE

Step by step

Bella Volen   Ulf Scherling

Colours: For this painting I used normal wet-colours, interference colours, gold and copper pigments mixed with mixing liquid, mosaic stones, blue glitter, mastix to glue the mosaic parts, sponges, painting brushes and body pencils. I knew exactly what I wanted to paint and how. I always write headwords about my idea, I draw it and paint it on paper. During the working process on the model I change some elements, but the main concept and composition always stay the same.

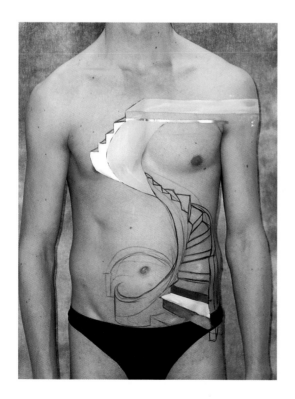

The drawing with body pencil. You see the most important part of the workstairs in the middle of the body. For me it is a symbol of the human and personal elaboration. You can always step up- it is your choice if you go up or down.

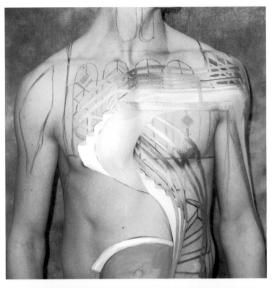

The drawing is ready and I have glued the first 2 mosaic stones. They are in orange on the left and right side. The fist golden lines from the parapet are done. He has a window on his eye- every one of us is an observer from a different perspective. There is also a small illusion with another window on his neck.

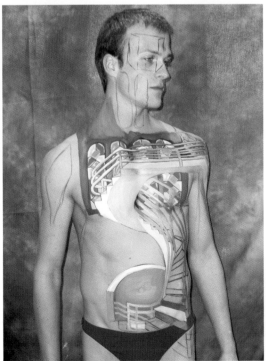

I painted the background windows in yellow, orange and red.I put some highlights with white on the "glass" windows, some black contours and grey around.

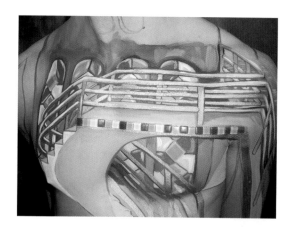

I glued some small stones with mastix on the skin already painted with gold.
I painted some dark and light lines around the golden parapet, so it will look more 3D, some blue on the narrow staircase.

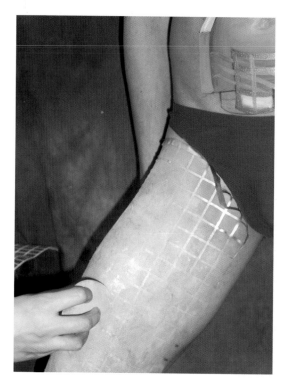

Using stencil and sponge for the stone structure on the "floor".

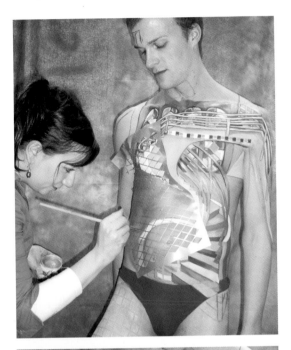

Using stencil, painting brush and interference blue for the "floor".

Sticking mosaic stones on the models leg and painting straight lines with copper.

45

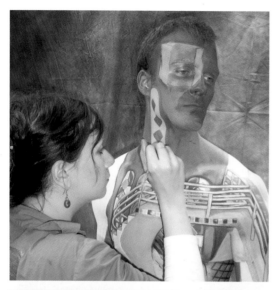

Painting a "glass" window on his neck.

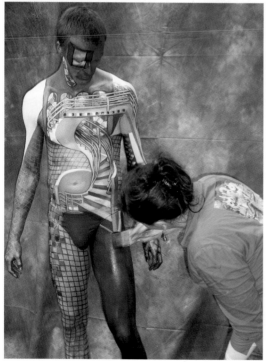

Painting a dark grey background on the models leg, which gives a contrast to the detailed work on the other part of his body. Now I have quiet and active parts of the painting. The viewer's eye needs a place to rest.

An Oriental Portrait

Step by step

Carolyn Roper   Brain Dicks

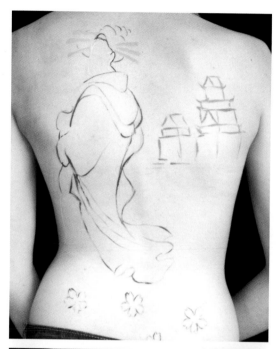

Paint the basic outlines of the design using colours that will be part of the final image.

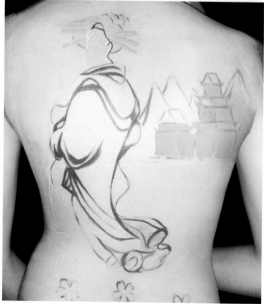

Block in the background colours and strengthen the main shapes.

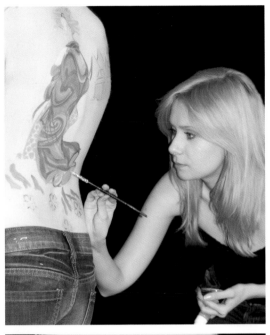

Fill in the focal points with the first layer of colour.

Add more detail, position the trees and start to work on the sea and sky

Add more definition to the sea, sky and mountains.

Start working on the finer details of the face, buildings and mountains and give more impact to the trees and waterfall.

Add the smaller details and shading to the geisha and outline all the main shapes in black paint using a fine brush.

Finished design

Deaths Head Moth

Step by step

Ernst Wieser   Ulf Scherling

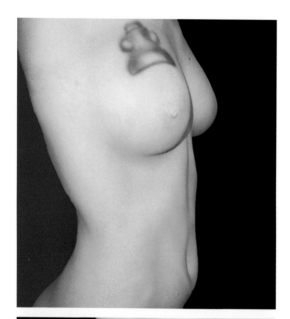

The shape of the moth, cocoon and caterpillar are airbrushed in one background
colour. Yellow for the caterpillar and
moth, copper for the cocoon.

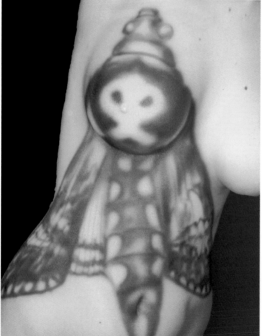

Details for the moth airbrushed in brown.

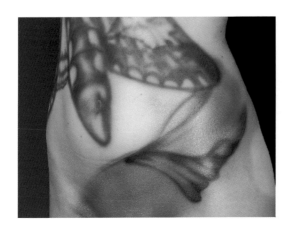

Details for the cocoon airbrushed in brown.

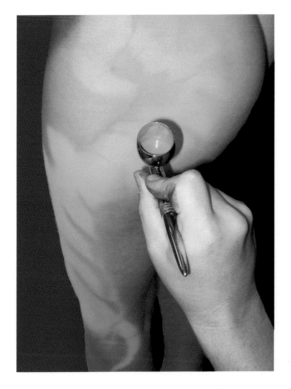

Details for the caterpillar airbrushed in green.

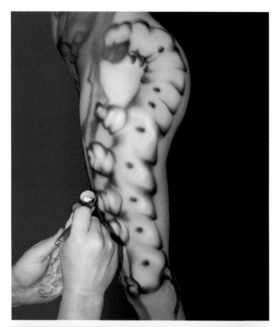

Adding structure to the caterpillar in brown and the stick it is climbing in brown.

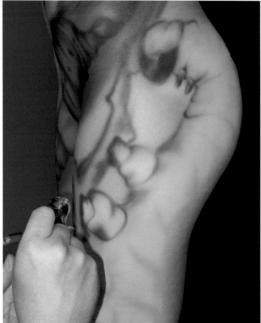

The moth, Cocoon and caterpillar are highlighted with white and shaded with black.

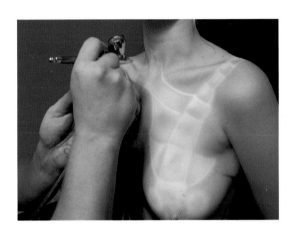

A ghostly moth airbrushed over the shoulder with a white base.

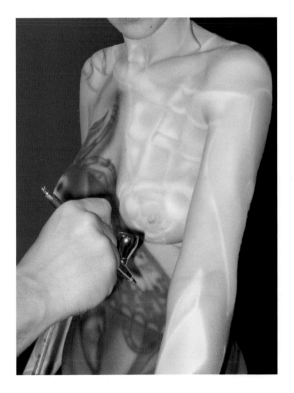

Structure for the ghost moth airbrushed in pale blue.

The ghost moth is shaded with black.

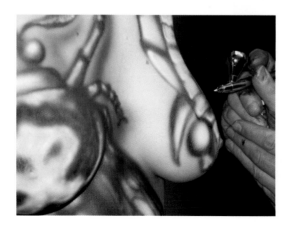

The showing skin is airbrushed copper for a finished effect.

Horned Devil

Step by step

Brian Wolfe

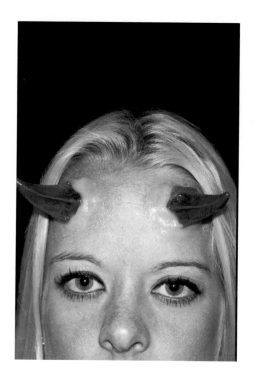

I started doing this piece with Heather Specht's personallity in mind. I got the idea for the hand in a tattoo magazine and decided to start with a pair of Scarecrow horns. These were secured in place with a children's glue stick. I used a fleshtone 2 part silicone to glob around each horn. While the silicone set up, I smashed the edges down with my finger dip-ped in isopropyl alcohol and stippled skin texture with an alcohol soaked sponge.

10 minutes later, when the silicone was dry, I based the whole thing by sponging her with light blue.

The shadows were layed in next with some dark blue and black.

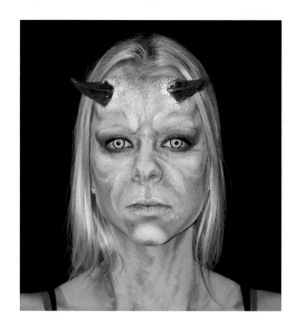

White highlights, contacts, eyelashes were next and the finishing touches were the silver ball on the hand tongue, to match her piercing and red paint on her tongue.

With the pictures finished, I moved on to the computer. I used Photoshop 7 and imported a picture of fire. I free transformed the fire picture till it was the same size of the portrait and dragged it over on top. Next, I moved the opacity to 50 percent on the fire so I could see her face through it and erased where I wanted her face and hand to show. I repeated the last step to get the flames on the bottom.

Alex Hansen

Step by step

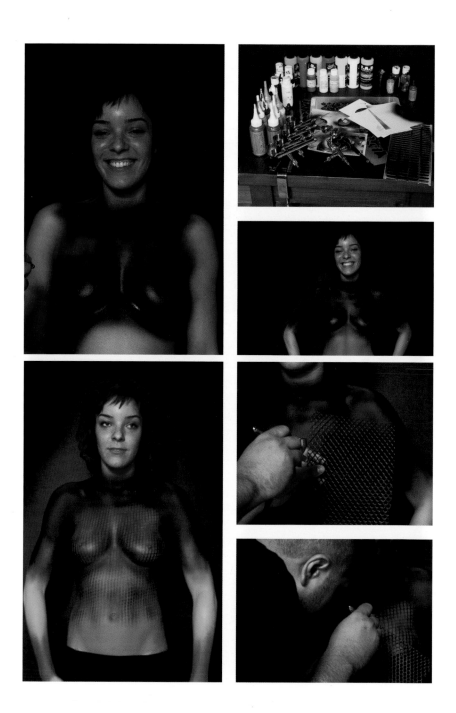

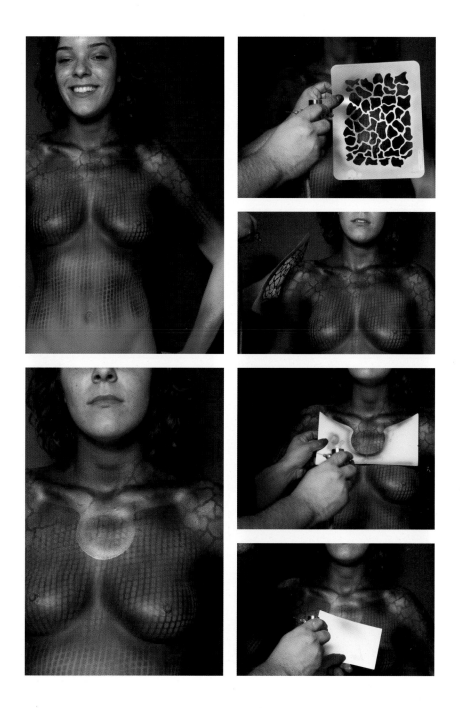

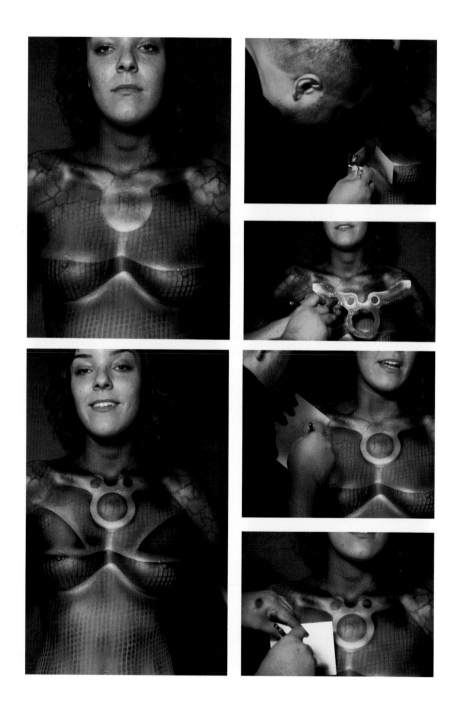

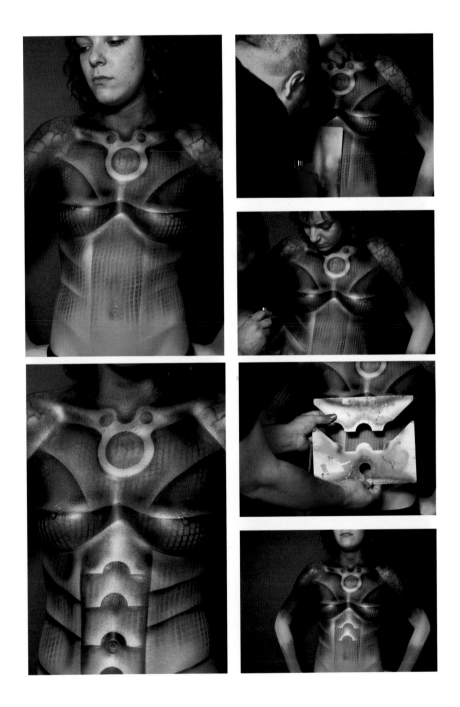

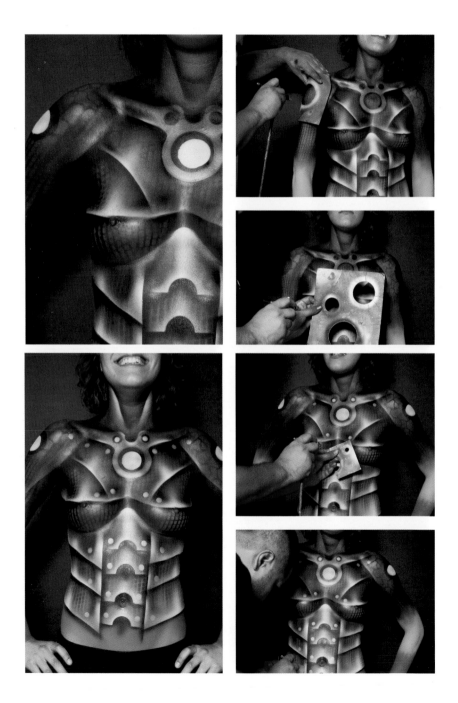

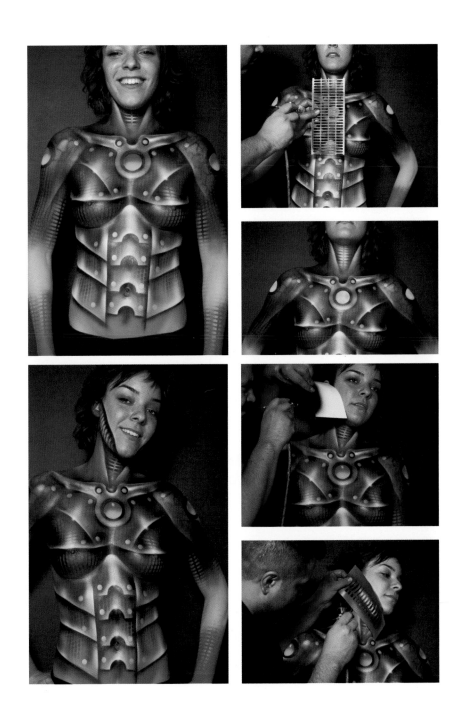

Brush & Sponge

In this technique the artist applies water colour or oil based paints to the body using sponges and brushes for general coverage, for blending and for details. In competitions painters in this category do not use airbrush or special effects.

The advantage of this style is that the artist does not need as much equipment as an air brusher, and does not need the preparation time that creating special effects requires. It is also possible to mix colours before applying them to the body. Covering the whole body and completing fine details takes longer with this technique. An artist working in this technique needs to have good painterly skills.

'I feel the brush as a part of my hand, as a sixth finger. I love very strong, powerful colours and I can only get the strong effect I want with this technique.' Bella Volen

'I like the various textures that I can get from a brush, whether it's in the stroke of the brush or the thickness of the brush. I like the sharp clean or edgy lines that I can achieve. I also like to use sponges, they come in different thicknesses and in a wide variety of textures.' Filippo Ioco

'Like any technique, it takes a lot of practise to get that smooth, evenly blended base and those crisp lines. Of course when you're working on a piece that's not for a competition, there are no rules and you can mix & match techniques to give the best effect.'
Raphaelle Feildhouse

Sebastian Langer from KRYOLAN presenting prizes at the
World Bodypainting Festival

KRYOLAN is one of the largest product manufacturers in the bodypainting
field. They have supported artists and the growth of bodypainting as an
art form with a personal and friendly hand, developing new products to
support the breadth of creativity and ideas that bodypainting artists have.
Founded in 1945, the company has served its clientele continuously
under one central maxim: to provide reliable support in the form of innovative, effective, and safe make-up preparations for make-up artists and
performers. More exactly: for the skin of performers.
Face and body painting artists have been especially successful in working
with KRYOLAN Aquacolor and the wide range of KRYOLAN products that
can be used when creating living art. If your line of interest is with the
brush and sponge, airbrush or special effects techniques, KRYOLAN are
the best place to look for the tools needed to create.KRYOLAN have been
a major supporter of the World Bodypainting Festival over the years.
They have made possible many of the innovations of the festival.

Aquacolor is a glycerine-based compact make-up, especially colour intensive, with the ingredients of superior-quality skin cream preparations.
Aquacolor is universally applicable, primarily as a make-up for painting
the face and body.

Application is effortless, with a slightly moistened make-up sponge or
brush. After drying, it can be gently buffed with a soft towel or with the
hand - but is not powdered. Setting spray is recommended if the make-
up will be subjected to extreme conditions.

Aquacolor is extensively smudge-proof and can be easily removed with
soap and water. Aquacolor is available in an extensive variety of more
than 360 shades, which include skin, vivid and metallic shades. Most of
these colours are available worldwide.

`I used to paint canvasses, so I was able to use the skills I already had
when working with bodypainting. I love the fact you can go from light
coverage to bold dense colours and brush marks.

There is often a little more to think about when planning out a brush and
sponge bodypaint design because of the way that the paints work and
the fact that it is difficult to paint a lighter colour onto of a darker base.´
Carolyn Roper

01 s	032	32 A	32 B	070	071
074	079	081	082	089	090
091	092	096	099	288	416
482	483	502	508	509	510
511	512	517	523	545	730
817	FF 7	G 56	G 82	G 83	G 108
G 176 A.	G 179	Gr. 21	Gr. 37	Gr. 42	R 19
R 21	R 27	P. 30	türkis	TK 2	T / weiß
altrot	blau 1	blau 3	blau 5	blau 10	276
man-darin	shatt. rot	gold	silber	kupfer	silber-grün

Another popular bodypaint is the iridescent water make-up, containing non metallic pigments, with pearlescent effects for creation of captivating make-up impressions on face and body. In addition to the classical colour nuances of gold, silver, copper and bronze, KRYOLAN offers a large assortment of vivid, iridescent colours.

One line of colours is designated Duo-Chrome. They reflect the light in a special manner so that the colours produce an opalescent effect. Interferenz wet make-up is available in single containers and in palettes.

"The shimmery colours are very special. They are a bit like chameleon and if you look at them from different angles are iridescent. The iridescence is caused by interference of light waves. The interference colours are created with glimmering particles of mica.

Unfortunately it is very hard to catch them on photo, but this makes them even more special. They remind me of unique nature elements- like a tropical fish, bird or butterfly or something from the future."
Bella Volen

Bella Volen   Ulf Scherling

In addition to a sufficient assortment of superior-quality professional bodypaints, along with professional equipment, a bodypainter must outfit themselves with the proper accessories to ensure successful work.

Essential in this kit are make-up brushes that satisfy professional demands: products with top-quality hair, first-class craftsmanship, functional design, and a good cost-benefit ratio. In short: brushes with outstanding quality. Here is a selection from KRYOLAN. These Professional make-up brushes are available in four models:
Round, Flat, Filbert and Angular.

"I love the way you can put strong clean colours over a large area so fast. You can paint really sharp dramatic lines with a conventional brush."
Raphaelle Feildhouse

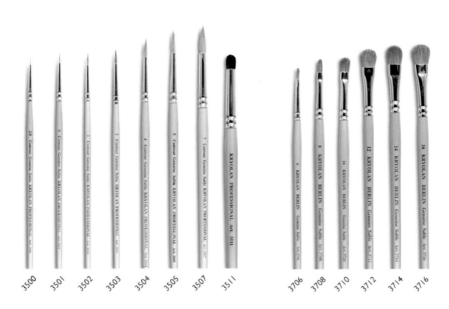

3500 3501 3502 3503 3504 3505 3507 3511

3706 3708 3710 3712 3714 3716

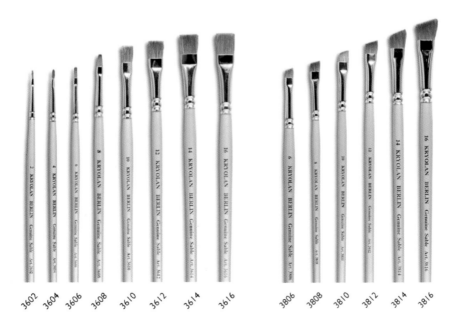

3602 3604 3606 3608 3610 3612 3614 3616

3806 3808 3810 3812 3814 3816

Presented here is a selection of superior make-up sponges from Kryolan. They are made of various materials and come in numerous forms such as natural latex, synthetic rubber, fine-pore synthetic substances, Nolatex, and natural sponge from the depths of the sea.

"I like to use sponges. Sponges are great because they come in different thicknesses and in a wide variety of textures, which can be very exciting once you learn how to manipulate such textures to your liking or to what you are trying to achieve."
Filippo Ioco

Bert Verstappen   Thijs Verstappen

Maurizio Luchetti   Gabriele Steiner

Airbrush

Artists working with this technique use an airbrush pistol and compressor to paint the body. In competition it is permitted to use a brush and sponge in this technique also. An advantage to airbrushing is speed. It is faster to cover the body and to create fine details.

The artist needs to take a compressor and airbrush pistols everywhere with them and the upkeep of these tools can be complicated and expensive. It is important to learn how to use the equipment, and time and practice are necessary. Colours used in airbrushing are also generally more expensive and the artist may need to buy a wider range as it is difficult to mix colours.

'Its benefits are its speed, smooth blending capability and ability to distribute paint on surfaces without direct contact with that surface. It's a difficult tool to learn. You need electricity and lots of additional airbrush related accessories in order to create.' Craig Tracy

'You can use universal techniques on the work surface or skin from fine lines to broad colour coatings. It's hard to find the best mixture of colour and thinner medium, water based or basecoats. If you've found the 'harmony' between paint and gun then you have a good chance to create.' Chris Oberheber

'You can paint on top of each coat, blending and at the same time mixing colours together to make a really nice transition. Shadows are also more realistic. With opaque colours you can cover over one coat. A very fine mist of light, gives that special realistic 3D accent.' Patrick Mc Cann

Udo Filon   Lex Hulscher

The airbrush has become a highly appealing application for the specialised make-up artist and bodypainter. Contact free application of paint with the almost imperceptible medium of air, along with the significant benefits that this method brings, have helped lead to a rapidly growing interest in this technique.

To successfully apply airbrush paint it is of course necessary to use specially designed equipment. Appropriate airbrushes, in addition to an effective compressor are essential.

"I got an airbrush on my fifteenth birthday and it felt somehow comfortable to me. I loved how it was allowing me to create. I practiced with it every day and within a year or two I was able to create paintings in hours that would take days with a traditional paintbrush. Airbrush defined the first half of my artistic career."
Craig Tracy

With these products and this equipment the artist can skilfully use the technique of airbrushing to achieve exceptionally uniform application of paint to face and body.

On this basis, it is possible to produce colour transitions with such gentle and softly-drawn appearances with perfect visual results, even for shots with high-definition camera technology. The chemists at KRYOLAN have developed a preparation just for these applications: AIRSTREAM Make-up Colours.

"Airbrushing is fast. You can paint on top of each coat, blending and at the same time mixing colours together to make a really nice transition from one colour to the next. Shadows are also so realistic and easy.

With opaque colours you can cover over one coat as easily as laying different coloured sheets of paper on top of each other without the other colours coming through to change the top colour. Making crisp lines with a stencil is no problem. You can spray a very fine mist of light to give that special realistic 3D accent."
Patrick Mc Cann

Chris Oberheber   Martin Moravek

Craig Tracy   Christopher Matthews

Alex Hansen   Carl Durocher

Special Effects Bodypainting

This technique is the combination of special effects with either brush and sponge bodypainting or airbrush bodypainting. All the rules of designing a bodypainting still apply, with the additional option of changing the underground shape of the body. Special effect attachments are generally made from latex and foam but can be made of anything you can think of.

It is possible to buy finished made applications or take a course in how to make your own pieces. This means making a cast of the body part, making a positive from this cast, building the special effects onto the positive and then again making a cast with the special effects included, and finally from this cast making the special effects piece. These special effects pieces can then be attached to the body before painting the constructed image.

It is necessary to take a course in special effects to learn how to make and attach these pieces. It is also important to know what is safe for your model and how to treat the model with care while using special effects. Once you have learned this then whole new dimensions are available to your imagination. It is still important to remember that you are painting onto the body so the special effects should be thought of as an enhancement to the artwork, not as a goal in itself.

There is a wide range of products available for working with special eff-ects. Almost anything can be attached to the body if it will not harm the model. Mastix spirit gum from KRYOLAN is a popular product for attach-ing effects to the body.

Special plastic and nose putty are also easy to use products that come in handy for realistic looking changes to the face and body. For more grue-some effects the blood products can also be used.

97

Patrick Leis   Gabriele Steiner

Martha Antal   Ulf Scherling

UV bodypainting

UV bodypainting can combine brush and sponge or airbrush. Fluorescent colours that glow under ultraviolet light are applied to the body. Bold patterns and designs create amazing effects to the eye and black paint can be used to make parts of the body disappear.

For a performance or for photographing a UV bodypainting it is important to have a dark presentation area. Any light other than ultraviolet will deaden the effect of the glow. Props and attachments can create amazing effects as the model moves. When photographing a UV bodypainting it is important that the model stay still. It isn't possible to photograph with a flash so the photo needs a longer exposure in the low light.

Kryolan have a range of intense Ultra Violet colours. They shine as day glow colours in normal lighting and intensify under UV lighting. These paints are fantastic for bodypaintings under studio conditions, for stage performances or for night shows. They are easily removable with soap and water.

Agneiska Glinska   Oswin Eder

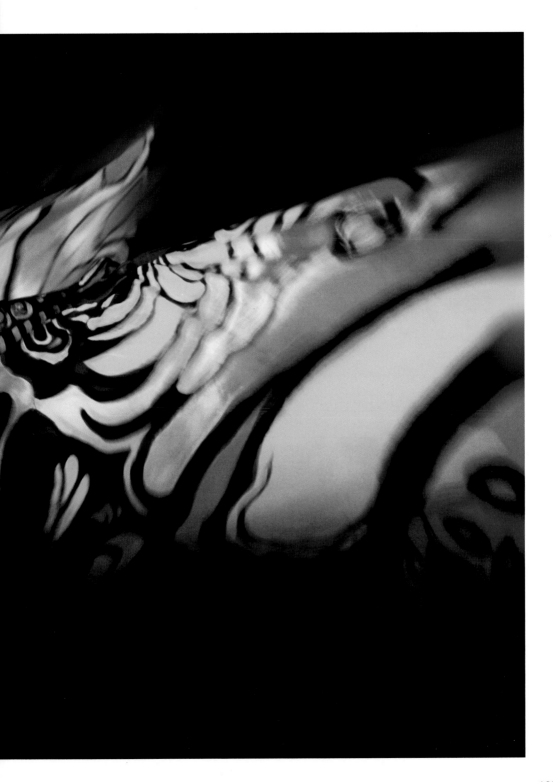

Bella Volen   Ulf Scherling

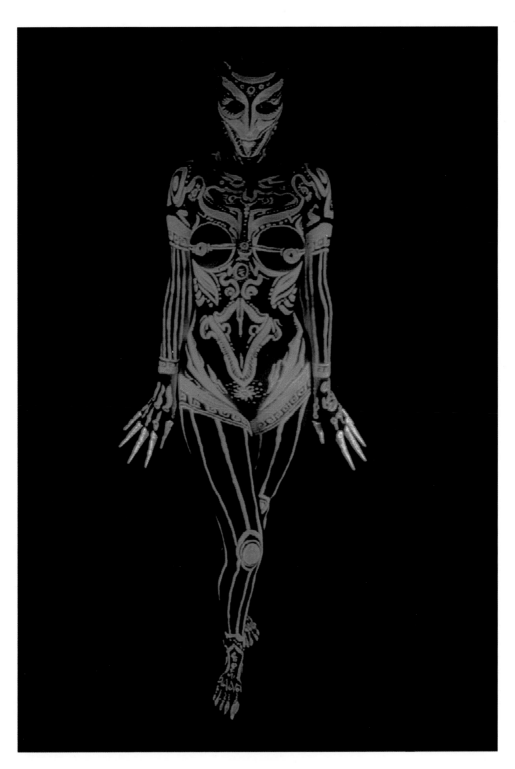

Wolf Reicherter

Fine Art Bodypainting

All bodypainting is art. Sometimes artists are working for a company or contractor and sometimes they are working for themselves. There should be no change in the quality of the work but there is most often a difference in the spirit of the work.

When a bodypainter is able to create purely for the sake of art itself they can channel their own muse and create a visual work of personal, political, social, racial, gender related or spiritual significance. This is where bodypainting reaches into the world of fine art.

There are no boundaries or rules that specify exactly what a fine art bodypainting is but it can contain a message to the viewer, be of personal importance to the artist and harmonize through colour, composition and execution. This is where a bodypainting artist can reach any height through purity of idea and expression.

Exercise

Create a bodypainting that has a meaning. Pick a political, personal or gender related issue. Design a bodypainting on paper that explores this issue. Be aware of your composition, colour usage and image usage. Set up a back drop for your bodypainting to be photographed.

Filippo Ioco

Filippo Ioco

107

Mike Shane   Thomas Karner

Gerda Fantina   Oswin Eder

Filippo Ioco   Filippo Ioco

111

Bella Volen   Bella Volen

Bella Volen   Bella Volen

Fashion

Bodypainting for fashion is there to complement and enhance the work of the designer. A bodypainter working in the fashion industry will work in collaboration with the designer, the photographer, the makeup artist and the hair designer to create the finished look desired by the designer.

The bodypainting will be confined to smaller areas of the body depending on the clothing, jewellery and accessories being displayed. The small area of paint may be intricately detailed or a simple line depending on the look of the shoot. It may be inspired by the fabric of the clothing or it may be a continuation of the jewellery or a separate pattern to compliment both.

It is important to consider the wishes of the designer. If the bodypainting is combined with clothing the artist should find out if it is ok for the paint to rub off on the inside of the clothing where it may touch and if not to find a way to protect the clothing. For a live show artists must take into consideration the movement of the model and clothing changes.

Working in collaboration with designers and makeup artists can be confining but can also offer opportunities to be inspired and to find new styles and directions.

Exercises

Pick a photo from a fashion shoot that you like. Redesign the fashion shoot with the addition of bodypainting.

Pick a photo from a live fashion show that you like. Redesign the fashion show with the addition of touches of bodypainting.

Alex Hansen   Carl Durocher

Alex Hansen   Carl Durocher

Karen Yiu   Ike

Filippo Ioco   Filippo Ioco

Karen Yiu   Ike

Advertising

It is important to consider the final result in an advertising bodypainting before beginning the first design of the work.

To be taken into consideration are:

Location. Is it an indoor still shoot in a controlled environment, a promotion in a shopping centre with all age viewers or a moving video? These variables determine the time available to paint, the needed durability of the paint work and the appropriateness of the amount of body exposed.

Product. Is it a company logo being advertised, a product or an idea? This determines the design and what it should include.

Contractor. Companies don't always have an understanding of what bodypainting can achieve or what it requires. Be sure to communicate with the contractor, be sure to have an understanding of their expectations and inform them of what is possible in the design plus all the practical aspects of creating the work.

It is still possible to create a fantastic artwork while following the needs and wishes of the contractor. An artist should be sure to use imagination and innovation, and to use your specialist skills to create an image more evocative than any that could be created by a digital designer.

Exercise

Pick an advertising campaign that you found inspiring and redesign the campaign with the addition of a bodypainting.

Pick a company or product and design a bodypainting including the logo of the company or product.

Filippo Ioco

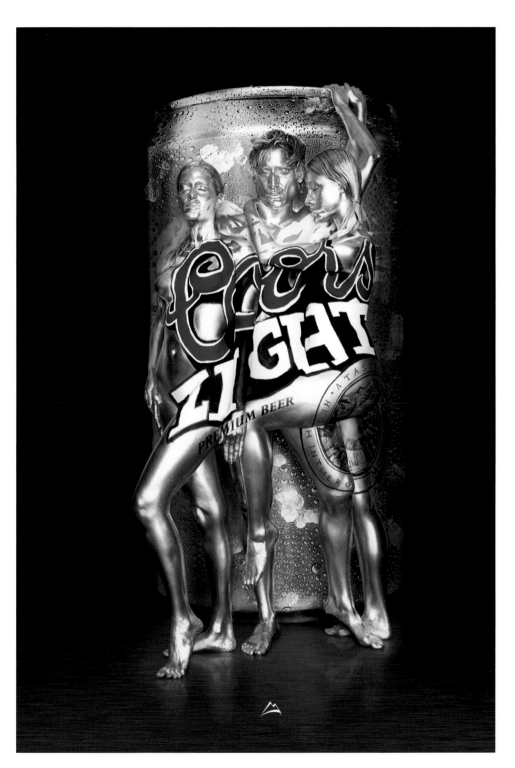

Filippo Ioco   Federick Algado

Filippo Ioco   Peter Gehrke

Mike Shane for CANON

HIGH-TECH.

neudoerfler
www.neudoerfler.com

EINFACH MEHR BÜRO.

Birgit Mörtl

I'll drink to that!

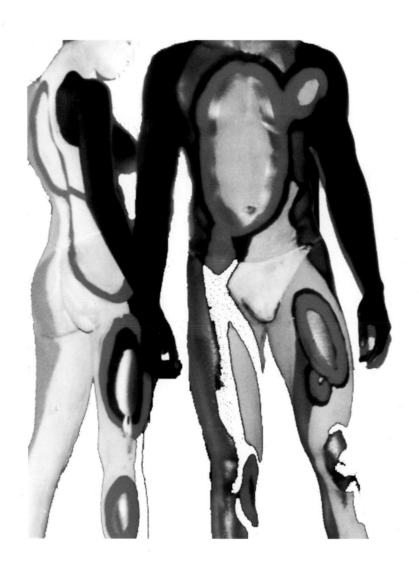

Filippo Ioco for BACARDI O

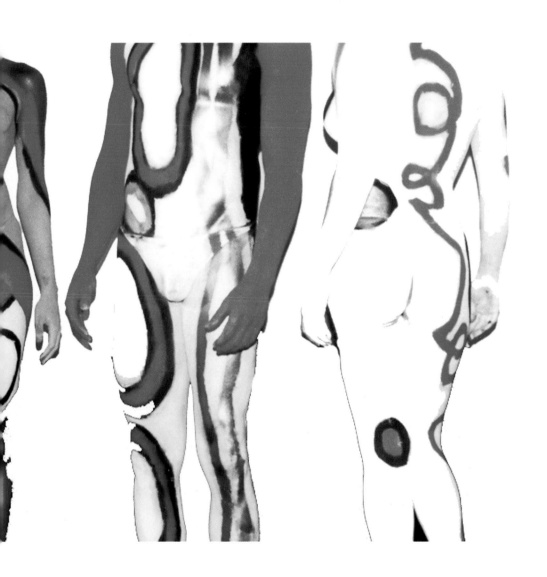

Competition

Painting for competition can be stressful but incredibly rewarding as it pushes an artist to bring together all their skill and understanding to produce a bodypainting that shows the best of their ability.

To be taken into consideration are:

Category. There are different rules concerning what is allowed to be used on the body depending on if it is a brush & sponge bodypainting, airbrush or special effects. Artists should know the rules.

Theme. Most competitions give a theme to paint to. The bodypainting should be inspired by this theme. Artists should think laterally and avoid the most obvious interpretations. It is always possible to interpret a theme and attach personal meaning to a design.

Time. Competitions have a time limit. Artists should practice the design they have created and be sure it can be completed within the time limit.

Personal ability. Every artist has strong and weak points. The bodypainting should display the talent of the artist to its best. It should contain fine detail as well as an overall harmony of composition.

Viewer. A bodypainting at a competition will be viewed by a jury, photographers and an audience. These viewers are placed at differing distances. A bodypainting should have an impact when viewed close up or from a distance, in a still photograph or in movement on the stage.

Exercise

Read the rules for the World Bodypainting Awards. Pick a theme from one of the previous festivals and design a bodypainting to interpret this theme.

Inese Deksne & Lauma Purvena   Gabriele Steiner

Maurizio Luchetti   Joachim Bergauer

Evgeny Koval   Thomas Badke

Bodypainting Models

Modelling for bodypainting is an art in itself. It is not beauty or fashion modelling, it is not only photographic modelling, bodypainting modelling takes a combination of talents that bring an artistic experience to life.

Ideally a bodypainting model should be someone, man or woman, with an expressive and changeable character. Someone who can take on the personality of the artwork they have become. Through eye contact, movement and expression, they should be able to relay the meaning of the artwork to the observer. A great bodypainting model can add extra layers of meaning to the artwork.

For the different uses of bodypainting it is also important to have the right model.

For a private artwork that will be photographed in a studio it helps to have a model with some artistic awareness who will understand the concept behind the painting. They should be able to pose well in front of the camera and have an understanding of their own body and how to carry it in relation to the artwork.

For a public bodypainting, such as advertising in a crowded place, it is important to have a model who is unselfconscious. A model working in public must be able to move past the fact that many people are looking at them, and to understand that they have become a living artwork.

For fashion and bodypainting the artist does not always have the choice of who will be their model. But ideally a fashion model who is being bodypainted will have something alluring in their character. Beauty is wonderful but even better is an intriguing persona.

For competition all of the above are necessary. In competition a model must stand still for around six hours getting painted, then be able to come to life in character to show the artwork to a jury, audience and photographers as if they are fresh and in character.

Bodypainting as an art form must include aspects of nudity so it is important that artist and model come to an understanding about this. Every person has a different comfort level. An artist must speak with their model and find out what their comfort level is and respect it. It is essential to respect personal boundaries while painting and not come into unnecessary physical contact with a model.

A model's privacy should also be taken into account when designing a work. A private bodypainting in a studio has less challenges as model, artist and photographer have control over the final images that will be viewed by outsiders so they can come to an agreement with each other about whether underwear is needed for the pose. Competitions and work in public require underwear on the model in most cases and in some cases nipples must also be covered.

Always ask first, there are a range of products available for coverage that don't interfere too much with the artwork. As a general rule though, the less you have to stick on a model to cover them, the less naked they look as the viewer then focuses more on the art itself as apposed to the distracting lines of slips or bras.

Tips for models taken from the World Bodypainting Festival

These tips are designed for models working at the World Bodypainting Festival in Austria but can be useful to all bodypainting models.

Modelling for a bodypainting is an amazing experience that can build confidence and open up areas of a person's character they haven't explored before. Any person can try it so use the opportunity to enjoy and explore.

Getting ready.
Remove body hair where necessary. Moisturise the evening before but not in the morning unless the artist specifies.

Bring - G-string, white without lace or decoration. A black G-string is better for a UV painting. Hair brush, soap and baby oil for hard to remove paint, shampoo and scrubber. Camera. Towel and clothes that can get dirty. Paper towels. Healthy snacks. CDs if needed for a performance.

Stretches.
Stretch well before painting time to start off with a warmed up body. This helps to avoid cramps and to stay focused. It is easier to pose after the painting is finished.

Through the day.
Try to keep the body as relaxed as possible. Drink water in small mouthfuls spaced over time. Drinking a whole bottle of water at once makes going to the toilet more constant. Keep muscles warm by tensing and relaxing them. Do mini stretches that don't disturb the artist. Eat food that will give energy but not be too heavy or messy. Fruit, muesli, light grainy bread can make good energy snacks. Sugar gives a fast boost but no lasting energy so don't rely on it all day. Energy drinks or energy lozenges are good just before going on stage or into the photography area but don't use them all day as they can also bring on a drop in energy.

Be aware of artist needs. Where are they painting? Is it a small detail? Can you move to help?

Do you already know your artist? If not speak with them about their idea so that you can prepare yourself for your performance and posing. Do they have music for you to dance to? Listen to it when possible.

Performance.

A performance should have a beginning, middle and end. Move in an appropriate way to reflect the body art. Be dramatic. Make eye contact with the audience, photographers and video crew, and interact. Enjoy it! Make every performance something to remember.

Photography.

Photographing the art work is very important as it is the only way to preserve body art.

Do a variety of poses that complement the artwork. Don't move too quickly as the photographers need time to frame their pictures. Listen to the camera flashes!

If the photographers are clicking furiously then it is a good pose. Keep it a little longer and try to make eye contact with all photographers.

Do small variations on that pose.

When the flashes go quiet then try something new. Make eye contact! Change facial expressions! Try poses that use a variety of levels and make it interesting. Use the ground, and the air, jump, fly, be alive.

Finishing.

Showering. When paint is difficult to remove, try baby oil. If the artist has used glues to attach things then they may have a specific solution to re-move the glue. Stretch again before sleeping to avoid waking up with a cramp.

Alfred Barangay   Peter Ziegler

142   Natalia Pavlova   Ulf Scherling

Jelena Velicko   Ulf Scherling

Nick & Brian Wolfe   Ulf Scherling

The World Bodypainting Festival

The World Bodypainting Festival with the World Bodypainting Awards was created by Alex Barendregt in 1998. Alex created an event to bring together bodypainting artists and show this little known art form to an audience. In the decade since the festival has grown into the world's largest and most important event in the bodypainting industry.

The 'World Bodypainting Festival' in Austria is a cult event that has encouraged innovation and provided a platform for hundreds of talented artists to further their abilities and careers. The World Bodypainting Festival is also a home where bodypainting artists have built up their own family.

The festival is set up over a week at the end of July each year, in the town of Seeboden, Austria.

The 'World Bodypainting Festival Academy' runs through the beginning of the festival week. This is a learning centre for people interested in becoming bodypainting artists and for practicing artists to further their skills. Workshops and classes are held with the leading artists from every field.

The three main days of the festival run from Friday to Sunday and are built up around the 'World Bodypainting Awards'. These are the world championships for bodypainting and are given each year in Seeboden in various categories. These awards recognise the most talented artists from around the world each year. The three main days also include an extensive music program with entertainment late into the evenings. On the final day of the festival the awards are given in a creative stage presentation ending in music synchronised fireworks.

The 'World Body Painting Association' (WBPA) was developed through the festival. This is an association for artists, photographers, models, schools, companies and product producers working in the bodypainting field.

Oswin Eder

The World Body Painting Association

The World Body Painting Association (WBPA) is the leading organisation in the development and support for the bodypainting art form. The Association began as a result of the yearly World Bodypainting Festival in Seeboden, Austria, and focuses on networking between artists, interested people and companies.

The World Body Painting Association is dedicated
-to promoting the art of bodypainting,
-to supporting artists around the world and
-to encouraging fair trade between artists and companies

The association looks after the interests of artists who have either made bodypainting their profession or who just paint for a hobby.
Photographers, models and video film makers are also members in the association.

The association is connected with schools, colleges, other communities and event organisers. Business partners and sponsors also stay in close contact with the association to offer its members benefits and to communicate industry information.

Benefits for members

Members of the association receive

-The official membership card each year
-Online presentation on the association's website www.wbpa.info
-An official members T-Shirt
-The right to use the logo in their website and printed matter
-Free admission or discounts to events and get togethers, supported by the WBPA
-Agency work free of charges
-Promotion for their own events and activities

-Only members can ask for the WBPA patronage for their own events and bodypainting contests. The WBPA patronage includes support from the association, help with organising, guidelines, agreements, advertising and more.

-Special discounts with the associations co-operation partners between 10-30% at online shops, product retailers for body and face painting, make-up, compressors, accessories, books, DVD's and other learning material as well as discounts with schools and colleges.

Other benefits include

-Free admission to the World Bodypainting Festival's grounds.

-Special discounts on festival shop products.

-Discount shopping on the festival grounds.

-Discounts on all workshops run through the World Bodypainting Festival Academy including the combined study courses.

The World Body Painting Association is present at tradeshows and events around the world. They also organise get togethers and encourage a social atmosphere among artists. For more information or to join up just visit www.wbpa.info

WBF Academy

Workshops and Grouped Study Certificates

Since 1998 the World Body Painting Association has organised workshops and classes with the world's best teachers in the bodypainting industry. For anyone wishing to take the first steps into this amazing art form, or take existing skills to a new level, the week of the World Bodypainting Festival ending in the World Bodypainting Awards has been the perfect environment to learn, be inspired and make the connections to get ahead in this booming industry.

Over the years the number of workshops and classes at the World Bodypainting Festival expanded to cover every imaginable need that an aspiring bodypainter could have. To recognise the hard work of our students and teachers, this learning week was reformatted and launched under the name of the WBF Academy.

To make choosing lessons easier, courses available through the WBF Academy are grouped into units. Grouped study certificates are also available for structured learning with a specific direction. These include 'Bodypainting for fashion', 'Bodypainting with Special Effects' or 'Bodypainting for advertising'. When booking three or more workshops a discount is given off the combined cost. Group courses are also available for existing schools wishing to include a WBF Academy certificate as part of their students training.

Unit 1 Foundation of Art
Colour theory, composition, light and illusion.

Unit 2 Techniques
Airbrush
Facepainting
UV
Brush & Sponge

Unit 3 direction

SFX

Bodypainting for Advertising

Combining Fashion Make-Up with bodypainting

Unit 4 surrounding knowledge

Beauty Make-up

Photography

Adobe Photoshop

Model workshop

Henna

Anyone wishing to take part in these classes is welcome. All teachers are leaders in their fields who work in the industry meaning that knowledge of techniques and products is constantly updated and cutting edge.

Grouped Study Certificates

For those people wishing to make headway into working professionally in the industry, an extended course with a final WBF Academy Certificate is available.

A WBF Academy Grouped Study Certificate is made up of three or more classes. One class from unit 1, one advanced class from unit 2 and one class from unit 3.

For example students wishing to work in fashion can take a group of workshops including Foundation of Art from unit 1, an advanced brush and sponge bodypainting or airbrush course from unit 2 and Combining Fashion Make-Up with bodypainting from unit 3. This would complete the units to receive a 'WBF Academy Grouped study Certificate for Bodypainting with Fashion'. We recommend students taking this course to have some prior training in make-up.

Similarly students interested in working in bodypainting with special effects can take Foundation for art from unit 1, an advanced airbrush or brush & sponge course from unit 2 and an SFX course from unit 3. This would complete the units for a 'WBF Academy Grouped study Certificate for Bodypainting with SFX'.

Students wanting to work in advertising can take a group of workshops including Foundation of Art from unit 1, an advanced brush and sponge bodypainting course from unit 2 and Bodypainting for Advertising from unit 3. This would complete the units to receive a 'WBF Academy Grouped study Certificate for Bodypainting with Advertising.'

Students are free to mix and match courses depending on the field they would like to work in as long as they meet the requirement of at least one unit 1, one unit 2 and one unit 3. Students may complete all courses within one week at the Academy, or over two festival weeks if they are returning the following year. Students may take all three courses from unit 3 if they wish.

Courses from unit 4 are not necessary to complete a certificate but also contain useful knowledge for anyone working in the industry. Anyone wishing to attach a course from unit 4 will have it noted on their certificate.

For more information about workshops look online at www.bodypainting-festival.com

Iconic Artists of our Time

In every art movement there are artists who lead the way in developing new styles and ideas.

Over the following pages we will look at the work of 24 artists working in countries all around the world in varying industries, whose work with bodypainting has and is settling the direction of bodypainting today.

These artists are the people who are breaking new ground, inspiring and influencing other artists. They are the foundation of a movement that takes ist roots in history but is as their imaginations.

Alex Hansen

Alex Hansen

www.alexhansenart.com

Alex Hansen is known throughout the bodypainting industry as a master of special effects imaging, and his airbrush technique and bodypainting style inspire many developing artists. He has produced hundreds upon hundreds of images that document his development. His creations range from elegant and delicate decorations to surrealistic images that mix the human form with mechanical shapes producing an organic robotic finish.

"I love the human form and I have a thing for making costumes. I always wanted to be a special effects makeup artist too so I mixed both together and love what comes out of it. It's a living canvas and it's great when the model plays with the ideas that I created on their body."

While many artists spend years perfecting the art of free hand airbrushing, Alex has chosen to follow the opposite path. After mastering free hand airbrushing, Alex turned the use of stencils into an art of its own. Alex may spend weeks designing and drawing the many small parts that comprise his creation before patiently cutting out the fine details of his stencils. These are then used within a few hours to create layer upon layer of colours creating sinuous and tightly designed images.

"I think I have matured as an artist. I'm still learning as I go, I still have much to learn, but I see the world differently than most regular people. I have a sense of appreciation for even the smallest details in everything and everybody's art and how people react to what I do and what other artists do too. When it comes to bodypainting, I feel I have the freedom to express myself more easily with the help of a great model, my work really reflects my inner creative child."

Some of Alex's most effective works are his collaborations with hair designers such as Alain Larivée and Eve Parr. Although the amount of actual bodypainting in these photos is minimal, what is there is designed in such perfection that the images are elegant and powerful. This is exactly the purpose of bodypainting when combined with fashion.

Some of Alex's special effects bodypaintings can be confronting in their gore and violence and can shock unsuspecting viewers. These scenes of mutilation and distortion created with living models showcase his ability to work in various dimensions.

Alex has created an encyclopaedic body of works encompassing a great variety of expressions. After years of dedication he is now sharing his skills through teaching and making his artwork available to a wider audience.

"I would love to travel the world, teach and learn form others and continue producing new and fun art for the masses. Books, calendars and images to inspire everybody at every age and culture. Then I can really reinvest in more and greater projects and imagery. I feel that my art is now respected for what it is and not how it is done."

Kathy Slamen

Peter Ziegler

Carl Durocher

Kathy Slamen

Carl Durocher

Jean Chouinard

Mark Thomas

Michel Bedard

Art Color Ballet

Art Color Ballet

Directed by Agnieszka Glinska

www.baletcolor.pl

Art Colour Ballet from Poland is a dynamic group of performing artists who have created some of the most amazing expressions of bodypainting. The group was established by artist and choreographer Agneiszka Glinska in 1998 with the idea to combine dance with the art of bodypainting. Over the following decade they have had a changing and growing company consisting of dancers, painters, and acrobats working together with artists and photographers to explore endless possibilities of living creation.

'With combinations of modern contemporary dance, classical, acrobatics, pantomime, afro dance and new forms of expression developed by the group we can get through to the audience on more levels, show them not only expression through dance but also tell them a story through lines, colours, shapes and images captured in designs painted on the dancers.'

Most bodypaintings originate from the idea of the painter. This ballet company add a refreshing and innovative touch to the bodypainting world as the ideas originate with the performers. The success of a bodypainting is dependant on the ability of the model to express the creation. With 10-20 highly skilled dancers and acrobats working within the group, they have an amazing level of control and understanding of what is physically possible for the human body. The borders between artist and model disappear within their creations.

`After some time, we also began using elements of painted scenography made by the artists in our group, as well as hand painted costume fragments and movable elements such as paper balls, carton boxes, and sashes. Fine Art Painting, bodypainting and dance are the combination of three of my passions. I was lucky to meet very talented dancers and artists without whom the group wouldn't have come to existence´

Art Colour Ballet is a unique group and has performed extensively throughout Europe and the world. They have been major contributors to the

World Bodypainting Festival since 2002 with artists Agnieszka Glinska, Joanna Cieśla and Anna Pogodzinska winning many awards in brush and sponge technique and UV effects. They have inspired other bodypainting artists to think about the wider possibilities that a living canvas can produce using performance and expression. Their dancers are among the favourite models for photographers every year at the festival with their images in the top ten of the world bodypainting photography award every year.

'It is our way to express the emotions evoked by the world that surrounds us. As we all see it differently, our shows also leave a wide variety of interpretations to the spectators. We are often surprised by the final effect of our work. We aim to synthesise music, dance and art in our shows into a coherent and inseparable entity to enable people watching the performance to be transmitted into the world of dream and fantasy.'
Agneiszka Glinska

Waclaw Wantuch

Ursula Eisl

Ulf Scherling

Franz Etzenberger

Johann Fenz

Joe Aichner

Franz-Josef Kollig

Bella Volen

Bella Volen

www.bella-volen.com

Bella is one of the most inventive artists bringing together her training in colour theory, composition, and symbology with illusory light to create imaginative compositions on muscle and skin.

Bella comes from an arts family in Sofia, the capitol of Bulgaria, and was raised among painters, sculptors, dancers and poets. She speaks fluent Bulgarian, English and German. Bella extended her natural talent with twelve years of formal study in some of the most prestigious art institutes. She studied at the fine art academy in Sofia followed by a fine arts master's degree in Vienna and has undertaken many private courses with well known international artists.

'At the beginning my body paintings were more decorative than a painting. Many of them were made for competitions. Now I am only interested in the creation itself. I was creating androgynous art and I still do. The difference is that now I work much more on the concept, the idea behind and I like to play with the space around, so the body will be a part of the whole atmosphere. At the moment I do not just paint on bodies. I do contemporary body transformations.'

An aspect of her work is its removal of sexuality. Using mainly male models her artworks contain genderless messages that call to both male and female viewers with the same curious invitations.

'I have three parts to me, Bella as an artist, woman and person. Only one of those is really female. The person and the artist are just thinking, feeling the energy river around and the creating process. So of course these parts of me like androgynous art. If God, the creator, doesn't have a gender, then why should art, being a creation, have a gender?'

Bella's painting on canvas reflects strong architectural interests. The building of walls and structures is symbolic for order and stability in human lives. Bella takes built structures and transforms them into optical illusions with light and colour to distort the realities of what surrounds the characters in her paintings. Her work challenges the viewer to take a leap into her passionate imagination, away from stability and order.

'There has always been good, amazing and also crappy, horrible or just bad hobby art. I think it is a lot like humanity itself. My biggest and most beautiful love could be hated or ugly in the eyes of another. But we are all humans and we all need love, it is the same with art, it needs to be expressed, enjoyed, loved or hated, free, but it has to wake up something in us.'

Bella's bodypainting work contains the same strength of visual messages as her canvas work, inviting the viewer to step out of their boundaries and think away from structured reality. She also works with UV and has won the World Champion title for her UV bodypainting. The intensity that Bella pours into her own artistic experience also flows into her collaborations with artists around her, as she travels to work on group projects and give support to other artists in their art making.

Bella Volen

Bella Volen

Kosio Kosev

Ursula Eisl

Bernd Ettinger

Rumiana Chapanov

Kosio Kosev

Birgit Mörtl

Birgit Mörtl

www.designfactor.at

The work of Birgit Mörtl shows a combination of mastered talents brought together to create an art form that stands alone. Birgit has worked for over a decade as a master tailor in costume design. She has explored all the techniques available in bodypainting. She has also studied and practiced the possibilities made available by special effects. The final artworks created by Birgit are a combination or costume, paint and special effects that are uniquely balanced in beauty, mystery and the bizarre.

As a master costume designer and maker, Birgit has worked for many well known theatre productions and musicals. This requires the ability to be in tune with the artistic ideas of a group and to create individual pieces that express human character in all its variety. Birgit works closely with the human form to transform her costume work, using bodypainting, to change an image more drastically than a costume can allow.

"I love to arrange a three dimensional body with colour and special effects, to transform it and dive into a fantastic dream. My work then begins to live through the movements of the model. On the body effects can be obtained which would never be possible on a flat canvas. I am dressing people, just like in my work as a costume maker. They do not feel naked. The model carries a dress manufactured by me, a breath-thin costume of colour."

In her bodypainting Birgit displays the same curiosity and will to learn that has already made her a success as a costume designer. She has spent many years attending every kind of workshop available in special effects and bodypainting.

"At first while bodypainting I painted with brush and sponge. Gradually I realized you can make interesting effects fastest with airbrush. I began to take more interest in airbrush and visited courses. Now I work with a mixture between airbrush and brushes. I have always been interested in special effects and body decoration. Next to one of my greatest passions, painting, I simply love to create things, masks, to build and construct them."

After some years of learning Birgit Mörtl reached the same level of mastery with her bodypainting as with her costume designs. Now she works successfully combining all these talents to create master works for fashion, theatre and competition. She is World Champion Bodypainter for Special Effects and has created bodypaintings for well known designers such as Donatella Versace.

Some of Birgit's most fascinating works have been for the Life Ball in Vienna, Europe's largest charity event. Birgit has been on the staff of Life Ball since 1997 and has played a major role in the creation of the 'style bible' each year. Birgit is an artist whose work has been at the hub of European experimentation with fashion and image.

"I would like to dedicate more time to my passion, bodypainting, in the future. I have so many ideas in my head that belong on the human canvas."

Gerhard Merzeder

Markus Morianz

Markus Morianz

Markus Morianz

Oswin Eder

Carolyn Roper

Carolyn Roper

www.getmadeup.com

Carolyn Roper is a talented bodypainter who works in the make-up industry. Her work covers a range of styles from fine, delicate beauty paintings to disturbing, body changing illusion work. As well as being one of the most requested artists through a range of industries, Carolyn is also one of the youngest and her work has progressed at astonishing speed.

After completing her make-up artist training and founding her own business in 2003, it took Carolyn just a few years to claim the World Champion title in the brush and sponge category at the World Bodypainting Festival.

"I was studying for my HND in specialist make-up when I read about the World Bodypainting Festival and thought it looked interesting. I had never painted a full body before and had no assistant, but I came 17th and decided it was something that I wanted to develop further. As soon as I started painting on bodies it just clicked. I like the way a bodypainting can tell a story and have a range of emotions. You can play with the lighting and the position of the model's body, your artwork changes every time the model changes position. Bodypainting is for me the perfect way to combine my art background and my make up training.

Standing on stage in Austria in 2007 after becoming one of the new world champions is a memory that I will cherish forever and I don't think any other experience in my career so far has come close to it."

In the short time Carolyn has been working as a freelance make up artist and bodypainter she has built up a client list that most artists can only dream of. Some of her most successful works have been for the music industry while working with artist Storm Thorgerson who is known for his surreal designs for Led Zeppelin, Pink Floyd, Peter Gabriel and many of the most talented musicians of our time.

"Every job I've worked on for Storm Thorgerson will be etched onto my

"Every job I've worked on for Storm Thorgerson will be etched onto my brain forever. The surreal nature of his photographs usually creeps into the photo shoot itself. Regardless of whether I'm painting eyes onto eyelids, turning someone into a jigsaw puzzle or painting a model in a white van on a freezing cold beach the shoots are always interesting, hugely challenging and some of the most satisfying jobs that I've done.

Music industry jobs are always interesting. I really enjoy working on CD album and single covers as I know that the design is almost always going to be something exciting. There really is nothing quite as thrilling as the first time you see your artwork on a 20 foot billboard in the middle of London, or walking into a music store in America and being able to pick up a copy of your own work."

Even though Carolyn has already achieved so much, her artistic drive continues to push her forward. She is World Champion, has her own make up DVD, her own business, teaches internationally, is internationally published, sits on juries for competitions yet still pushes herself to develop in new directions.

"I think as an artist it's important to keep pushing yourself. I think there is so much more to be done with body art and I never want to stop learning."

Gerhard Merzeder

Ulf Scherling

Rupert Truman

Hass Idriss

Joseph Sinclair

Joachim Bergauer

Oswin Eder

Tim Regas

Chris "OBSN" Oberheber

Chris "OBSN" Oberheber

www.obsn.com

Chris Oberheber is one of the leading airbrush artists in the bodypainting field. His technical dexterity and creative ingenuity are reflected in body-paintings that combine aspects of futuristic fantasy with sharp edged interpretations of life today. Working on every surface from bikes to bodies, Chris has a recognisable airbrushing style that is high voltage with a touch of humour.

'When I began to discover the advantages of working with an airbrush pistol I also awoke a great curiosity in trying out every surface as canvas, including skin. It was a decisive moment when I decided to follow the attraction to artistically glorify the human body.'

There is a close understanding necessary between the three aspects of creation in a bodypainting. Artist, model and photographer need to have clear communication between each other to create finished images that stay true to the original intention of the work. Chris works closely with photographer Martin Moravek and model Mike Davis for many of his artistic projects and has a talent for harmonizing ideas.

'What could be more beautiful than being allowed to use a breathtaking body as your canvas? But you should never misunderstand this. It is always necessary to respect your living canvas. This trust between model and artists results in truly harmonious artworks. The model is our basis, our sculptural canvas.'

Chris plays an important role in the bodypainting community and his experiments push boundaries. He has won many awards at the World Bodypainting Festival for his airbrush work. He creates illusions with images and can create the impression that multiple living beings are playing over the one body. Chris' work is poetic and evocative, he is a magician of the industry.

'It's important to constantly shake up your own boundaries, to sharpen' technique and to try out new and unknown things. Thanks to the festival I see artists being able to measure their abilities as greater talents are constantly being displayed in the various categories. I see us as trend setters. Bodypainting is a constantly growing cycle that has grown into its own life form, ever more colourful, more bizarre and more demanding.

You are only as good as your last creation. My motto is never rest on your success. Strive constantly towards perfection, it is an obsession.'

Martin Moravek

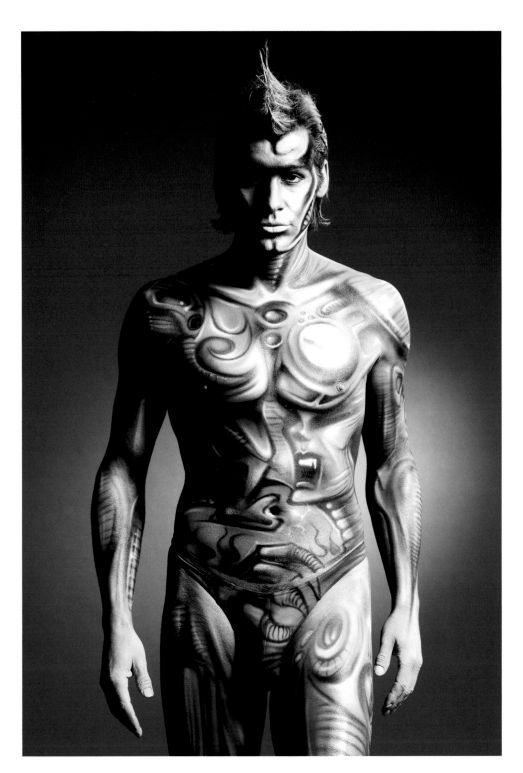

Martin Moravek

Martin Moravek

Martin Moravek

Martin Moravek

Martin Moravek

Craig Tracy

Craig Tracy

www.paintedalive.com

"My paintings are like songs that I sing only once but that I listen to for a lifetime." Craig Tracy.

Craig Tracy is a master airbrush artist, painter and sometimes even finger painter. He combines his work with both the living form and traditional canvas art to create illusions in fine detail. His compositions demand a perfect placement of the body that harmonises with the natural shapes present and reflects his appreciation of human beauty.

"I have been a professional artist since the age of 16. I have never had any other type of work at all since then. I lived and breathed art and sadly enough I was never truly satisfied with the art that I was seeing or creating. I felt like there must be something, something more interesting to create. The act of painting on traditional, conventional surfaces was utilitarian and I need more than the same old boring canvas, paper or wall to work with. I thought what if I painted on us? What if I SERIOUS-LY painted on living, breathing live human beings? Nothing even comes close to painting on people. People are my passion. Diamonds and gold are dull by comparison."

Craig Tracy became an important part of the bodypainting community when he joined the World Bodypainting Festival in 2004. He immediately found a place among an artistic circle of friends that has encouraged communication between artistic styles. He also further earned the resp-ect of fellow artists and bodypainting appreciators by becoming world champion in the category of airbrush bodypainting.

Craig helps spread understanding for the art of bodypainting to its view-ers by bringing together artists with varying styles and techniques. Some of his most interesting work is in collaboration with fellow body-painting artists. The idea of turning artist into artwork and creation into companionship is beautifully reflected in his works with Carolyn Roper and Britta Herold. These artists from different cultures and continents have travelled for miles to come together and create onto each others' skin. In these images the connection between artists to artwork and artists to each other is poignant and moving.

"I hope to write, lecture and continue to collect the work of other Bodypainting artists. Ten years from now I'd love to be able to look back at these first few years of my career and know that I was in the right place at the right time and that the work that I created somehow affected a positive shift in the art of Bodypainting."

One of Craig's greatest achievements has been the creation of the 'Painted Alive Gallery' in New Orleans. This is an innovation for the bodypainting world as it is a space dedicated purely to bodypainting.

"I've opened the very first gallery in the world dedicated exclusively to the fine art of Bodypainting images. I'm very proud of selling Bodypainted images and getting such images into people's homes and business as printed art. Being accepted into so many lives artistically is truly a wonderful feeling."

Christopher Matthews

Craig Morse

Christopher Matthews

Christopher Matthews

Georg Kuchler

Carolyn Roper   Georg Kuchler

Christopher Matthews

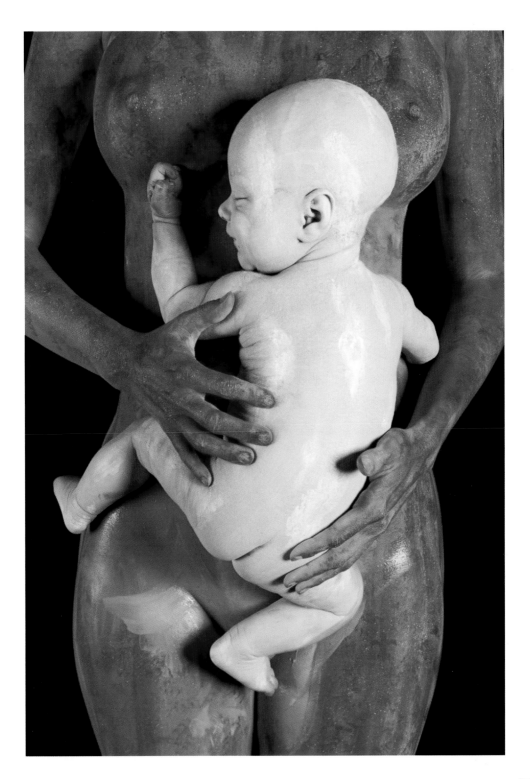

Einat Dan

Einat Dan

www.einatdan.com

Of the bodypainting artists emerging from the make-up industry today, Einat Dan is one of the leading artists exploring the possibilities of combining bodypainting with fashion make-up. With a combination of precision, elegance and a touch of the bizarre her creations hold the perfect balance between beauty and fantasy that can't be reached by make-up artists working with traditional make-up products alone.

In her bodypainting work Einat heightens the shapes of her model with intricate patterns and fine details. Her work tells a visual story that can be followed over the shapes of the skin with boldly balanced colours.

'I love to use the curves and the shape of the body in my painting, when you paint on canvas, you don't have to finish your art in the same day. In bodypainting you must, it's more stressful and more exciting.'

Already a successful make-up artist and bodypainter in Israel, Einat took the bold step of moving to Milan, one of the fashion capitols of the world. This move paid off with Einat coming into closer contact with an industry that allowed her creativity to explode. In fashion and fantasy make-up artists have the freedom to transform their models into more than daily beauties. They create a realm where the lines and shapes of the face can be cut, exploited and heightened to extremes.

Bodypainting is at its best in the fashion industry when the artist knows not just where to create but where to hold back. Einat's most successful works are those where a minimum of paint is combined with a wide variety of non-conventional materials to create simple but evocative images.

'In bodypainting you must use colours. In fashion sometimes you have to use colours and sometimes the opposite, it must be the most pale and sick make-up or half and half, but for sure in both you must be creative.'

236

Einat's portfolio contains a wide range of high profile shoots with well known photographers, designers and models. While working in collaboration with these artists she has managed to hold true to her own style and to make clear statements through her art. The world of fashion has only seen the beginning of what is possible when it is combined with the art of bodypainting.

'I wish to create more and more. I wish to create every art story and every picture I have in my head, in fashion make-up, fantasy and body-painting.'

Allesio Cocchi

Allesio Cocchi

Lene lindahl

Remo Forcellini

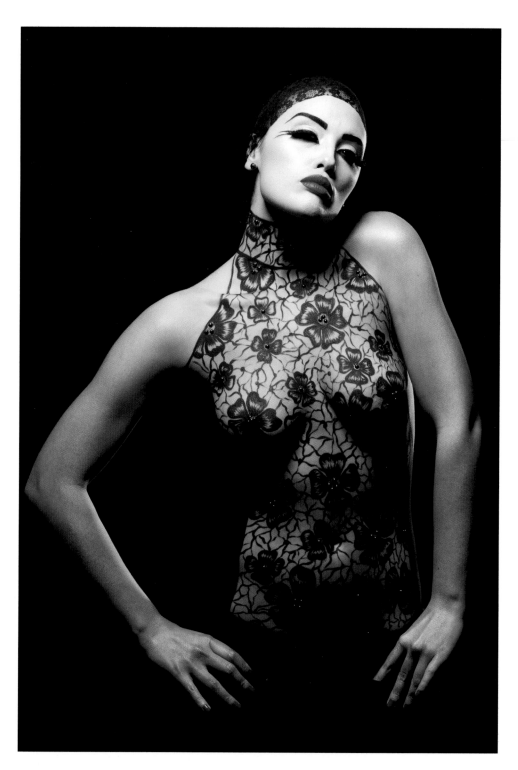

Yossy Ioli

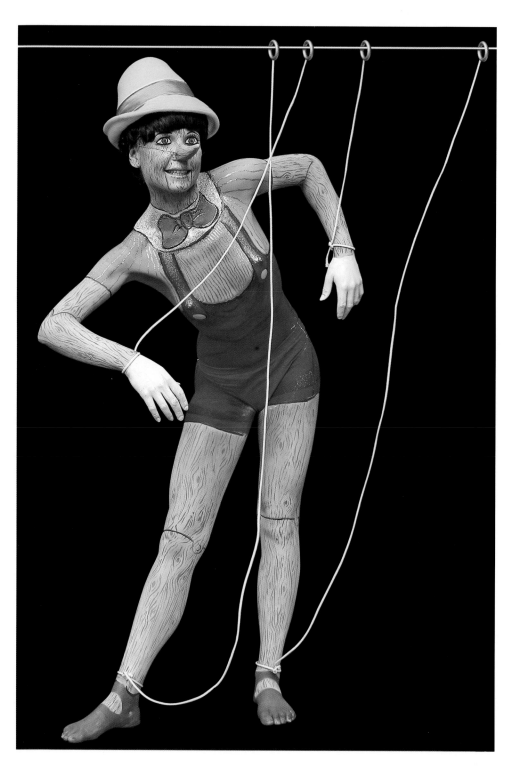

Steven Kratochwill

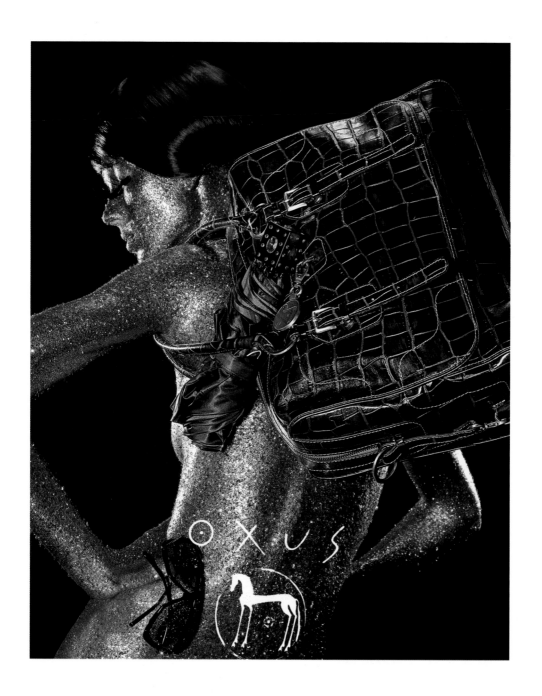

Erika Harrison

Erika Harrison

www.AmerikanBodyArt.com

Erika Harrison is a dedicated henna artist continuing a tradition that reaches back thousands of years, and reinterpreting this beautiful art form as a modern day expression. Her work incorporates elements of traditional technique and design with innovative modern methods.

"Traditionally, henna is used for celebrations, such as weddings and festivals. The most well-known tradition is the Night of Henna, or the "Mehndi Party" that is celebrated two days prior to a wedding. Henna is still used for weddings and festivals with people of Middle Eastern, Asian, and North African cultures, but thanks to media coverage of celebrities using henna, it has become quite popular in western cultures as well.

We mostly find henna being used as a long-lasting temporary tattoo. People get the same designs that they would get in a real ink and needle tattoo...minus the pain and permanence. Now that women tend to celebrate their changing bodies during pregnancy, I have been fortunate enough to henna many pregnant bellies. I have even had colleagues who hennaed women's heads who have lost their hair due to chemotherapy."

Erika is also a talented business woman and has found that difficult-to-reach balance between artistic expression and financial stability.

"As I became a body art instructor, it became necessary to start selling supplies to my students. Many body art supplies are so specialised that they can not be purchased in local shops unless you live in a very large city. I started out with henna supplies and then moved into glitter tattoo supplies. As I attended each new convention or tradeshow, I would discover a new product that I wanted to carry. Coming "from the trenches" so to speak, I understand the needs of the body artist and have always tried to develop products that would make their lives easier and their businesses more lucrative."

Most importantly Erika is a gifted teacher who travels to share her knowledge around the world.

"It was a dream come true when I realized I could make a living by combining my passion for body art and my passion for teaching into one career. I always tell people that I may not be the greatest henna artist in the world, but I am the greatest henna teacher in the world. My ultimate career achievements have been seeing my former henna students become fabulous henna artists."

Erika has a wide range of products available for henna art as well as beauty make-up. Her work has been featured in all the major magazines for body art and she continues to teach around the world at major conventions and festivals.

254 www.scottwatt.com

Ernst Wieser

Ernst Wieser

www.malerei-wieser.at

Ernst Wieser is an airbrush artist who has developed a style of fluid free-hand painting that goes hand in hand with his strong connection to nature and his desire to explore and invent. Ernst is one of the originators of the bodypainting industry and has devoted years of his life to develop the form.

A cherished face at the World Bodypainting Festival in Austria, Ernst has worked as the head of the Jury for the World Championships since the beginning of the competition over a decade ago. He has helped develop the process of the competition to ensure that artists have the opportunity to showcase their work fairly and to the best of their ability. His work with the festival has taken him around the world to teach and to help promote the festival.

'My work with the World Bodypainting Festival drove me to push myself harder with my own art making, to develop my own style of painting constantly and to be sure that my abilities continued to grow personally as an artist and a teacher or jury leader.'

"When not working on the festival Ernst runs with a large decorating company and specialises in interiors, special illusion painting, specialised airbrushing and custom paintings. His freestyle airbrush art has developed to a point of excellence".

When airbrushing freehand, without stencils, every stroke is like a signature from that artist that is unique and can't be copied. I have developed to a point where I don't need to do sketches or designs on paper before I paint. I can see the image and know instinctively how to create it from start to finish. This takes years of practice.'

Most of Ernst's art is inspired by nature. His free time is spent extreme mountain climbing. Over the years Ernst has climbed Kilimanjaro in Tanzania, Grossglockner and the Karnish Alps in Austria, the Julian Alps in

Slovenia, the Dolomites and Ortler in Italy. He has also travelled through wilderness areas of South America, Asia, Europe and Australia.

The speed of his lifestyle and the range of his travels are reflected in Ernst Wieser's art. He depicts nature at is strongest and finest, its fragility and its power. He is an inspiration as a teacher and role model to artists around the world.

Oswin Eder

Oswin Eder

Oswin Eder

Oswin Eder

Ferenc Hottya

Ferenc Hottya

www.artofcolours.at

Ferenc Hottya was an intense man, whose life flowed through many extremes of high and low, ending far too soon on the eighteenth of January
2007. His talent as an airbrush artist is highly respected and received the
highest awards.

Just six months before passing away Ferenc was standing on a stage with
an audience of thousands receiving the title of World Champion Airbrush
Bodypainter. Among that audience were many of the artists who he
counted as his friends.

Ferenc dedicated his life work to perfecting his talent as an artist, but
more importantly he dedicated his time to connecting the community of
bodypainting artists who were spread out all over the world. He app-
roached artists with a warm heart and invited them to join together
creatively. His passing has left a legacy of work and many fond memories
for those who miss him deeply.

"We see Ferenc as a pioneer of the bodypainting scene as he was in Seeboden long before our first participation in 2002 and was always faithful
to the family. We are amazed by his work still today. As with the festival
and some good artists, Ferenc's work and talent grew over the years.
Ferenc was and is a treasure for the bodypainting kult. His work will live
on."
the brushers

'Ferry lived so modestly, always helping others and giving, even if just
something small. As modestly as he lived, so modestly and politely he
went from us. So many ideas were not yet realised - so many words were
not yet expressed. Ferry gave me so much and also made changes in my
life through his urgent ideas and observations.'
Fredi Schmid

'He introduced me to a new world that he had helped develop. This world

was made up of an international family of Bodypainters creating and celebrating together annually, during The World Bodypainting Festival. Ferenc acted as a bridge, connecting individuals, talents and passions. My life was positively altered by this experience. Ferenc is responsible for so much of who I am today. He became my Brother. I miss him deeply.'
Craig Tracy

'Ferenc was like a friend of many lives past to me. I hope that I will run into him again in the next one. He was and will always be a great man, artist and friend. See you soon old Friend!'
Filippo Ioco

'One of my most memorable experiences would have to be my last combined work with my dear friend and 'big daddy' Ferenc, which makes this art form so honest and profound for me. You're in my mind and fill my heart with art.'
Chris Oberheber

Karin Landl

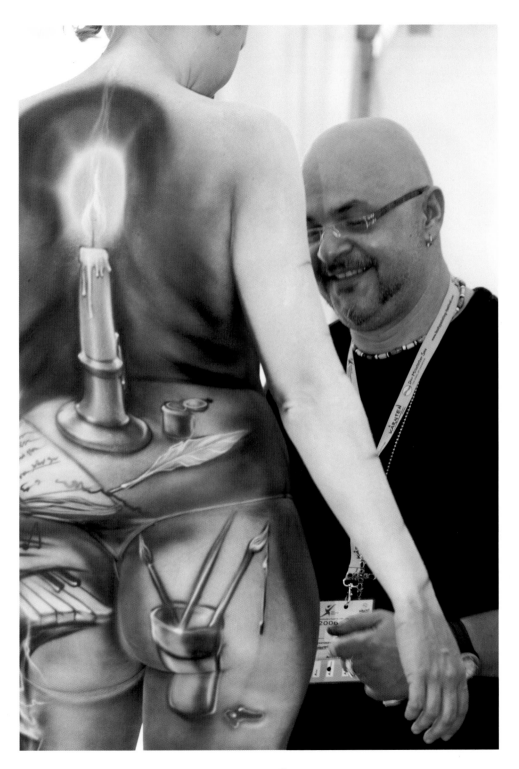

Karin Landl

Karin Landl

Uwe Nauland

Filippo Ioco

Filippo Ioco

www.iocoart.com

Filippo Ioco is one of the most outstanding bodypainting artists alive. His groundbreaking work covers an extraordinary range of styles and ideas. His combination of experience, understanding, inspiration, innovation and courage has kept his work at the top for almost two decades.

"Professionally I've been body painting for 19 years now but I've been a Fine Artist / Painter most all my life. I am able to carry that knowledge, technique and style over into my body art which sets me aside from other body painters. I've always wanted to work with the human figure but never really knew how until one day I thought of painting a body into one of my canvases and from that day on I became a body painter."

Filippo's work explores gender roles, sexuality, and perceptions of male and female shapes. He has placed the painted human body in every imaginable environment from natural to artificially created environments to frame his ideas.

"I have always been fascinated with the human body and nudity. I believe that it is truly the first form of art. We all come in different shapes, sizes and skin colours. I think that we should all be proud of our bodies no matter how big or small. Every body has its own beauty."

His advertising portfolio contains some of the most successful combinations of body art for the media. His work has been featured in music videos, on book covers, on television commercials and in the printed media. Filippo also dedicates a large amount of his artistic energy to charity work.

For those lucky enough to get the chance, watching Filippo paint live is like connecting with creation itself. His performances and models are spontaneous and alive. The documentation of his artwork through photography and video is lasting evidence of a long career of talent that continues to evolve today.

"My life is all about art, colour and visual stimulation. If you were to take away art I would be gone as well."

274

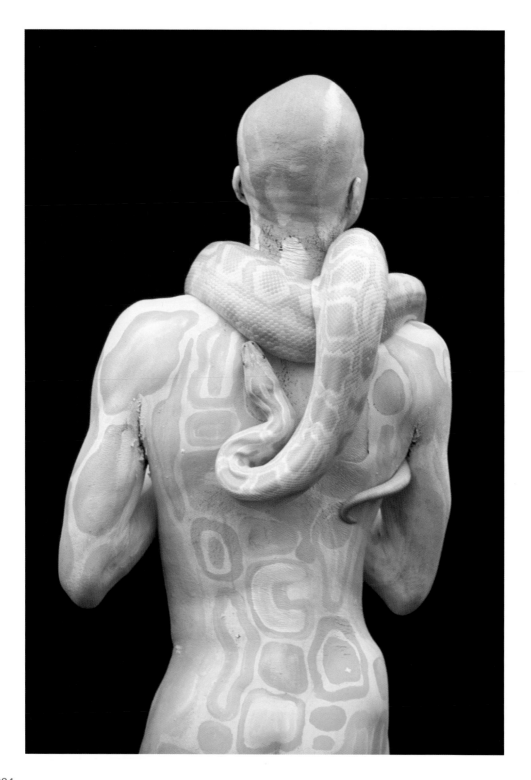

Fredi Schmid

Fredi Schmid

www.bodypaint.ch

Fredi Schmid is known for his ability to transform bodies into living art like pieces of a jigsaw puzzle. He is one of the key figures in the international bodypainting community and has worked for decades to further his innovative techniques and create an impressive portfolio of work. His ideas have strengthened the community of bodypainting artists and he has helped many artists find their own style and place.

'I first discovered bodypainting more than 30 years ago when I saw a report about Veruschka von Lehndorff. I still admire her work today.
I began by studying hair dressing for theatre which contained the basics for theatre make-up. I then studied further with courses in make-up art as it is used for film and television and an intensive bodypainting course in Crete.

In the beginning I made simpler motives with sponge and brush. With time I discovered airbrush technology, which made new designs possible for me. Particularly while participating in different competitions like the "World Bodypainting Festival" I decided to incorporate special effects into my work.'

Fredi holds many titles and trophies and his artworks express his years of contemplation and study of this art form.

'Bodypainting is not just about painting a picture on a body - Bodypainting is the coloured representation of today's life and the spirit of our time in fantastic form. The current generation is a short-lived, momentary one, "rather today than tomorrow". Everything must be fast and varied.

Bodypainting symbolises this thought in the sense of momentary art. It is only in one place for a short time, can not be held or reproduced again in the same framework. What you see live with your own eyes stays in memory as a visual event in the way it was experienced, live. My work has nothing to do with painting erotic zones, but integrating the human forms into a spatial picture. The body is a living three-dimensional canvas that constantly changes and can be totally different depending on the angle you view it at.'

Fredi has a generosity that spreads throughout the body art world as he shares his friendship, his knowledge and his ideas. Through his many personal projects and through his support and cooperation with fellow artists he continues to test his own boundaries artistically and be the catalyst for the creative development himself and of others.

Helmut Müller

Helmut Müller

Ulf Scherling

Georg Schmitt

Yves Verduyn

Gabi von der Linnepe

Gabi von der Linnepe

www.vonderlinnepe.de

Gabi von der Linnepe is a visual artist painting on canvas who discovered the art of painting onto the body by coincidence and has since developed into one of the leading artists painting for competition. Her work is centred on the illusion of the 3D shape carrying multiple living beings and creatures networked together.

'During my holiday in Seeboden I decided to go to the photo exhibition where the bodypainting artworks of the year before were shown. What I saw was absolutely fabulous. I immediately booked a workshop, bought 6 colours on the festival ground and went home with the latest video. I contacted my brother Marc and my sister Anne as models, my husband Stefano as second painter and my brother-in-law Markus as photographer and video man. I watched the video, developed my very first body painting and we went to the festival in 2004 very doubtful if we could manage to do a total painting within 6 hours.'

When working on canvas Gabi paints images from nature with bold patterns and strong colours. She has carried these themes over into her bodypainting work. Her bodypaintings take the body parts of her model and transform them into separate living creatures that then come back together as one organism. She incorporates this living art into a still background painted onto canvas creating a giant and ever changing painting with a dancing foreground.

'For me bodypainting is totally different from canvas painting. While canvas is a flat basis, the body has very different parts that should be considered in a good bodypainting. The painting can move, dance, and talk to the spectator and therefore the model is a very important part of the painting. As every body is different, the painting is very special and unique and it is always a challenge to create a new body painting design. To paint on a human body is really exciting and gives me the possibility to create new artworks that did not exist before at any time. I like to complete the art work by painting the backdrop and make the model part of a complete work of art.'

Artists who design their works to be filled with the human canvas understand the importance of having a model who can express their work creatively. Gabi often works with her brother as model and the unity of her painting with his expression and movement is highly successful on stage and in photographs.

'One of the most important things is to show people the worth of body art. I want to show high quality art - not a naked body with some colour on it. Therefore I prefer to paint on male models as I can be sure that spectators are interested in the painting instead of the beautiful naked (and unpainted) model.'

Gabi paints mainly for competition and has won many international awards for her work including second place in the brush and sponge category of the World Bodypainting Festival. She has a talent for interpreting the theme she is given in a way that still stays true to her individual style of painting.

'Since we began bodypainting we participated in several festivals in different countries and were quite successful. We got faster and also learned more about the colour, the possibilities, and the important or unimportant things for our creations. We learned a lot during the last years and are still keen about trying new things to increase the work and widen the range of possibilities.'

Friedrich Jamnig

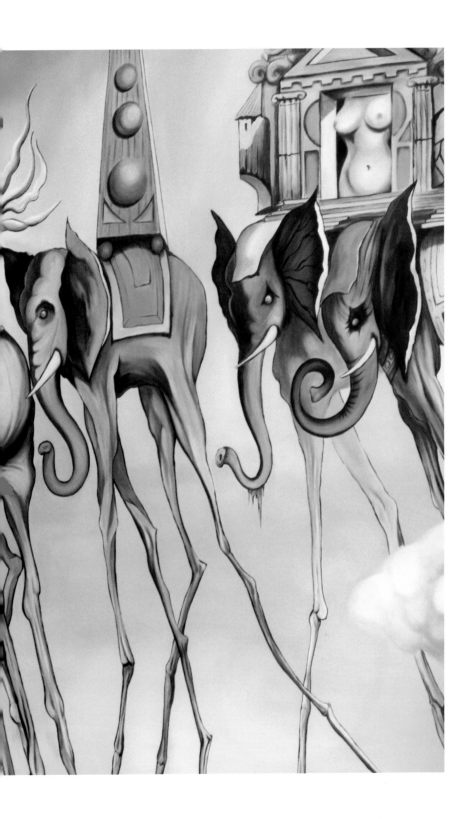

Harry Laub

Rüdiger Küfner

Oswin Eder

Gabriela Hajek-Renner

Gabriela Hajek-Renner

www.specialmakeup.at

Gabriela Hajek-Renner has taken bodypainting with special effects a step further and created a category of work that could be called living sculpture. Gabi's striking creations are evocative and theatrical. Her artworks are massive, detailed constructions turning the human body into organic architecture.

Gabi's talent is the result of natural creativity with years of study and practice. At the age of 15 she was already assisting her mother in an international competition for bodypainting and one year later created her first bodypainting alone while completing her training in cosmetics. She has since taken on a wide range of further study and is certified as a make-up artist, hairdresser and wig maker, mask builder and nail art designer. She has also studied the making of and application of special effects. All of this experience comes together in her bodypainting.

"The human body is something completely special. It is such fun to simply let the body flow into a painting, to partly change or completely change the body through attachments. I also paint gladly on paper or canvases, but one cannot compare this to working with the body. The necessary preparation often lasts for weeks so that in just a few hours I can transform the body completely into one artwork. This whole work lives then only for a short moment on the stage but the memory and photos remain."

Gabi's family play a large role in her creations. With her mother she has a cosmetics school where students can also learn the art of facepainting and bodypainting. Her mother works as Gabi's assistant when she takes on larger projects such as her competition work for the world championships, and even her son has played a special role in many of her artworks.

"The most important experience in my art making was the world championships in Seeboden 2005. I created the piano artwork which I constructed from two women, and my son who was six years old at the time played the role of Mozart in his first performance. Not only did we get the maximum points possible from the jury, we also received the public prize and won the world championships in special effects for the first time."

Gabi has won many titles and awards over the years. At the World Bodypainting Festival in Seeboden she has won fourth place, third place, second place and twice first place in the special effects category. She has also won third place in the facepainting category and fourth place in the UV awards and many other awards in international competitions for body art and beauty arts.

"I am always pleased that people know and remember my artworks. There is still so much art that I want to make. My personal style is always developing further."

Oswin Eder

Rudolf Mayr

Oswin Eder

Oswin Eder

Robert Nykodym

Genevieve Houle (Jinny)

Genevieve Houle (Jinny)

www.jinnymakeup.com

Genevieve Houle, known internationally as Jinny, has been a major influence on the style of bodypainting that has evolved out of facepainting. She has a degree in art and is President of Jinny, Make-Up Artiste Inc., Co-creator of Paradise Make-Up AQ, Mehron Advisor and Chief MakeUp Artist at Cirque du Soleil Special Events.

'Once I started doing artistic makeup the canvas would get a little bit bigger, face, neck, shoulders. It didn't take much time for me to start painting full bodies. I find it very challenging to create on people. When you start painting on a flat canvas it's always the same when you begin. When you use the body, it's always different because everyone has their own shapes and different features. I love painting on people because I enjoy the mixed combination of art, expressions and emotions.'

Jinny's brush and sponge technique combines art nouveau swirls with punk rock colours. Her designs are graceful and robust. Jinny creates eye-tricking illusion paintings with speed and accuracy. This is extremely useful when working with a time limit. Most importantly her designs work with the shapes of the body she is painting in fluid and natural created shapes.

'Because my art has been my full time job for many years now, I've had many opportunities to make my art grow. I feel like I'm working much more with the lines of the bodies. I look at the bodies differently now compared to when I started. I see shapes for each part of the human body and it makes it easy for me to create illusions. I compare the body to a big "puzzle". The image on the "puzzle" is the art on the body. Each piece is a human part and once you put them all together it flows and it's beautiful.'

Jinny has travelled throughout Canada, Europe, the USA and Australia to share her skills in bodypainting. She is a valued contributor to conventions and events around the world.

'Since I began to do body painting I've always promoted its worth artist-ically. I want to make people forget about the nude body underneath. I want them to enjoy the whole creation all together. I not only judge others in competitions, I judge what I do each time. I want to improve every day. I want people to see my artwork and to recognize my "signature".'

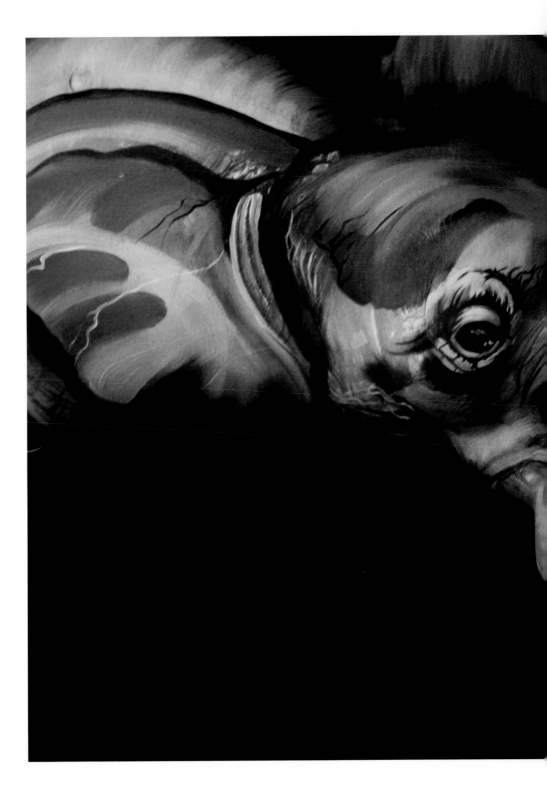

Karen Yiu

Karen Yiu

www.karenyiu.com

The art of Chinese-born Karen Yiu is rich, delicate, and innovative. Karen has created her own amazing collection called 'Body embroidery' with hand sewn embroidery placed directly into the make-up. Karen's journey to becoming a bodypainting artist has crossed as much physical space as it has taken time and practice.

Her journey began in Hong Kong where she moved at the age of six. Karen had finished a degree in social work and on a whim took up a make-up course with a Parisian tutor before moving to London where she studied at The London College of Fashion and came in contact with body art.

"When people see my work, they can see a Chinese influence, the drawing skills are influenced by Chinese painting, and I was educated in London. I have a more modern way of thinking, really east meets west. When I am creating my work I always look at some Chinese painting or handicraft for reference, 5000 years of art has loads undiscovered elements, there are some points only Chinese can understand. Chinese is a unique writing system, it's difficult to learn, if you want to discover Chinese culture you need to understand Chinese first. I hope to link up our history with body art. I want to make a difference."

Karen has travelled from Hong Kong to London, through Europe and back to Hong Kong. Along the way she has produced a volume of work combining asian and western culture, traditional painting styles with modern, fashion with body art and innovation.

"I do water colour, oil paint, different art forms, but body art is very different. I have to do it in a very limited time, the body is alive and it can move. I can see the audiences reaction instantly, when the photographer captures it, it will become a different art piece again, I can see the body art changing all the time. I like it with soul and I want to see the instant effect. Working with a photographer I can again produce one more art piece. When I am making my own art I just follow my mind, I am free to work however I am thinking. I don't need to predict how people will react.

Body painting combined with fashion is a good entry point for most people to understand what body art is, when they see these interesting images they would like to see more, this is a very good introduction for art. When I work with fashion I need to have a clear understanding what the fashion designer is thinking, how I can make up the painting to cooperate with the clothes, it is not only art but also a supplement of the fashion itself."

Although comparatively new to the industry, Karen has already produced a wide range of work that incorporates new ideas and a unique style. Her drive as an artist and her instinctive creativity is building bridges between the make-up, fashion and bodypainting industries.

"People always ask me, 'why do you do body art, don't you think this is difficult to make money? Do you think Hong Kong/ Asian people will accept it?' I tell them I don't care, I am an Artist and I am working with my art work, not money making work. I can make money by doing some simple smoky eyes makeup, natural wedding makeup, but I need art to make my brain survive."

Brigitte Weishäupl

Ike

Ike

Ike

Irena

Mike Shane

Mike Shane

www.bodypainting.at

Mike Shane's style of bodypainting is exhilarating and potent. His creation of the 'action painting' style is an innovation and a breakthrough. The technique remains his alone, as he works in the 'now' to colour moments of space and time. His work brings together all the necessary aspects of bodypainting: painter, performer, photographer, with such clarity of vision that his artwork is unforgettable.

'When I started my Action-Paintings bodypainting things really changed in my life. Everything shifted and moved into a different level. I had recently gotten to know tompho.to, a brilliant Viennese photographer. After a certain time of working with him I realised, that the topping of a good Bodypainting was a good photograph of it. This was basically the start of a new view and new outputs of my work.'

Mike has studied fine arts and in his performanced work with athletic models whose movements are elegant and intriguing. Mike's radical liquid splashes of colours contrast with each other on ever changing levels as he composes, changes and destroys his fluid orchestral arworks. His works also celebrate the movement of paint with gravity, how fast, where and why it will move a certain way over the shapes it reaches.

'My work is fully intuitive. I have to reinvent myself every time I body-paint. The most interesting part for me is keeping the body line "alive". I found out pretty fast that I didn't like to paint "pictures" on the body. I found my challenge in doing abstract paintings. And it always fascinated me that once the body moves 2cm the whole concept needs to follow and change. Also the texture of a body is different to ANY other surface. It has soft parts, "under boned" parts, straight lines as well as tricky angles.
All in all it's really thrilling!'

Mike has created an impressive portfolio of work for advertising and promotion. Some of these works are carried out in his action painting style but many of them show a separate angle to his work that is equally creative. Mike is able to take the logo or idea of the company he is contracted by and to design it into a bold pattern of colours that lives on the body. These bodypaintings are equally important as they show that it is possible to create a commercial bodypainting and still have an artwork as a finished product.

'I want to reach even more big internationally known companies to work with bodypainting as a business, marketing or advertising tool. I want my Action-Paintings to take place on big event-stages all over the world. I want to show people how powerful colour can be. How strong its effect is on our minds. How harmonic it can be combined with music, dance and visual arts.'

Thomas Karner

Thomas Karner

Thomas Karner

Thomas Karner

345

Thomas Karner

Nick and Brian Wolfe

Nick and Brian Wolfe

www.eviltwinfx.com

Bodypainting in the USA has grown out of the face painting and clown industries. Brush and Sponge bodypainters in the USA often work with bold colour combinations and designs that follow the structures of the underlying muscle and bone structures. This bold approach contrasts with the fine lined delicate work seen in artists from other continents who reached bodypainting through the make-up industry.

The artist brothers Nick and Brian Wolfe are at the forefront of this body-painting style and have driven much of the development of the form in the states.

Just as in more traditional forms of art, one of the first steps an artist takes is to study the anatomy of the human form. When drawing an arm, the artist must have an understanding of the bone structure, where the bones fit together and bend, where the muscles are attached to the bone and where fat can pad out the surrounding areas.

This understanding of anatomy assists any artist working with the light and shadows that highlight the bumps and shapes of the human body. Artists who draw and paint on the human form create moving sculptures with light, colour and shade.

Nick and Brian have taken this step in mixing anatomical knowledge with living art. Their anatomical understanding is put to creative use in their dissections of human form and transformations of reality into the physically impossible.

"The human body is the most beautiful thing to us both inside and out. Painting a 3-D image on a 3-D canvas creates a new dimension in our eyes. When it is brought back to a 2 dimensional medium with photography, it is hard to tell what reality is. One can focus on the image, see right through the painting or take in both."

The most recognised artworks from the brother team would have to be their fantastic monster creations where flesh, muscle and bone are ripped, exposed and contorted. Other artworks created by Nick and Brian use special effects to reach into the realms of fantasy and character. Their artworks are all the more powerful as their composition always balances and explores the shapes of the living model beneath them.

"The constant need for more and more and bigger and better is the human condition I think. With my art I compete against myself and always strive to do my best."

Nick and Brian now teach workshops in bodypainting technique around the world. They have an infectiously positive outlook on life that flows through their art. Important in their life and art is "a remembrance of who we are and who everyone else is. Global unity, respect and recognition of this art form."

"We share all our tricks and techniques and in turn, our students share with us. We feel we will never stop learning or evolving."

Peter Rabl

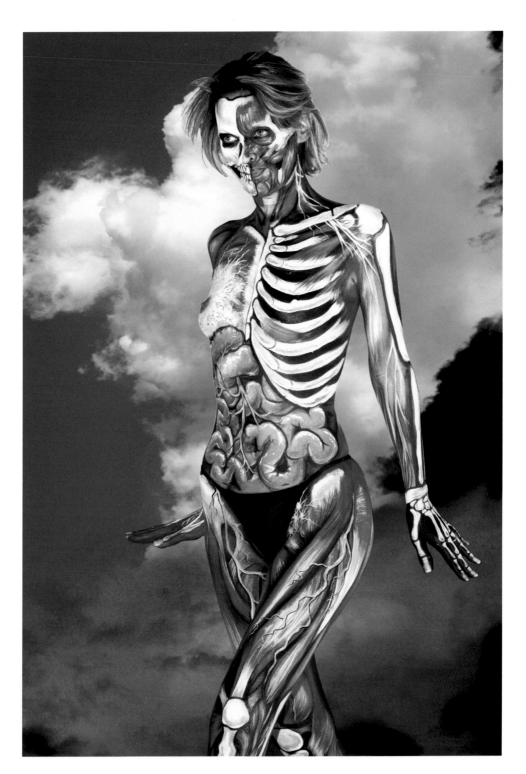

Gerhard Koller

354

Rich Johnson

Raphaelle Fieldhouse

Raphaelle Fieldhouse

www.raphaelle.co.uk

Raphaelle Fieldhouse is a master in brush and sponge technique. Her compositions on the human body are visually beautiful bringing into harmony the physique of the models she chooses with the complex ideas she likes to transmit through her art. She is one of the most awarded bodypainting artists and runs a successful entertainment company named 'Body Canvas' with her husband Gary.

'Since starting Body Canvas in 1999, I have had more goals to aim for. I practise many forms of art including bodypainting. I enjoy drawing, painting and sculpture but the living form has so much more to offer an artist than a lifeless canvas or board. The whole process is collaboration between artist and model and once the work is complete it truly comes into its own. The painted shapes and patterns are distorted by the movement of the model's body, changing the character of the design and literally bringing it to life.'

Raphalle's natural talents are supported by a wide range of study and practice. With diplomas in art and design, make-up art, theatrical and media make-up and wig making, she has dedicated years to perfecting her skills. After directing her artistic energies into bodypainting she used competition painting as a way to push herself further. She has since twice been awarded World Bodypainting Champion in the brush and sponge category in Seeboden as well as many first and second places at most major competitions around the world.

'What ever I do, I always try to do the best possible job of it. If you're going to do something, do it properly. So I entered many different competitions to push myself to be better. I have learnt a lot along the way — not only about bodypainting but also about photography and how the permanent image is presented. My work is growing and I'm always looking for new ideas to explore.'

Raphaelle has become a respected artist within the body art community and has received global attention from the print media and television. While continuing her entertainment business Raphaelle has also moved into teaching and passes on her experience to students around the world.

'As well as bodypainting I am also trying to be a part of the more conventional art scene with collaborative exhibitions and projects. I would like my bodyart to be appreciated not only within our own genre but by the wider art world in general. I don't think that bodypainting is an equally respected art form as other media. I would like to produce purely creative pieces and to be able to sell the photographs as finished works that hopefully people will want to have on their walls.'

Thijs Verstappen

Reinhard Bichler

Guido Simons

Chin Clinton

Sarah Bull

Sahra Bull

www.vaig.com.au

Sahra is a successful make-up artist based in Sydney, Australia and working internationally. As head make-up artist from VAIG studios she has had years of experience in creating make-up for high profile clients, teaching and guiding the direction of a creative make-up team in one of the busiest fashion industries. Her work with the studio has been featured in top fashion magazines, music clips, fashion shows and advertising campaigns.

Sahra's work combines beauty and spirituality with a feminine strength that makes her artwork stand out from other artists. Sahra's skills as a ballet dancer, painter and make-up artist, give a grace and sensitivity to her living art.

Sahra has a deep interest in the culture of the goddess. She has travelled the world winning awards. She has painted in Dubai, throughout Europe and many Asian countries. Along the way she has made a detailed study of representations of the female and goddess art in traditional cultures. This is then channelled back into her bodypainting creating living goddesses.

'I choose to paint the 'Living Form' as being an artist and having studied make-up, the combination of the two was a natural progression. Painting on soft, pliable skin is quite different to a rigid canvas and therefore to paint well and expressively is a real challenge. This challenge presents itself over and over again to me as new works are designed and created.'

Being a visual artist, Sahra has an understanding of composition, colour and symbology in art. As a make-up artist she understands how to translate these elements onto the human body in fine detail while using the shapes and character of her model. Finally, as a trained dancer, Sahra understands the possibilities available to a living form when composing the final shot or performance for a bodypainting.

'My most memorable achievement in Body Art would have to be becoming The World Body Painting Champion of 2005 and with that honour, having met so many wonderful people along the way. My art has definitely grown over time. I feel that my work has matured as I have matured.'

After a short break from the spotlight to become mother to a tiny goddess named Kiana Ngaere (Kiana meaning literally moon goddess) and to live her dream of cutting ties with city life, Sahra returned to her work as make-up artist and bodypainter.

'It remains to be seen how my work will further develop. I hope to be able to continue creating many more beautiful artworks for the rest of my life.'

Klaus Gaggl

Chin Clinton

Dan Freene

Oswin Eder

Gabriele Steiner

Gabriele Steiner

The Brushers

Udo Schurr and Patrick Mc Cann

The Brushers

Patrick Mc Cann and Udo Schurr

www.the-brushers.de

The vibrant team made up of two talented airbrush artists is known as 'The Brushers', Patrick Mc Cann from the USA and Udo Schurr from Germany. They live in Germany, work throughout Europe and have made an international impact with their work in the bodypainting field.

Their work is technically flawless with fine detailed free hand airbrushing and compositions that reveal conceptual and poetic interpretations of themes. Their individual and combined work has won the highest awards including two times World Bodypainting Champions for airbrusch and two times vicechampions.

When given a theme to interpret, The Brushers always come up with an idea that surpasses the obvious interpretation. Their work challenges, provokes and confronts. Their work often contains political themes yet with positive insights for the future.

"We like to make collages. To melt many different ideas and impressions together to make the person looking at the artwork think a little. The idea grows and then we melt the idea together to fit around the whole body. It's sometimes the provocation of ideas that are maybe too sensitive for some people. That's the beauty of art. To make a person think. It's not always pretty."

Patrick and Udo's analysis of life and their drive to inspire people to see a positive future is also reflected in their position in the bodypainting community. By staying in contact and being a constant presence at international gatherings they have been able to inspire the artists around them and generate their ideas to a world audience.

"We are impressed by how Bodypainting has grown so far. The World Bodypainting Festival has changed the direction and the reputation of bodypainting. It is now an accepted art form to be used in everyday life. It also brought so many different types of bodypainting art together and is now really amazing. So many artists have helped to bring bodypainting to a high level that can be seen anywhere, it is an expression that lives."

Ursula Eisl

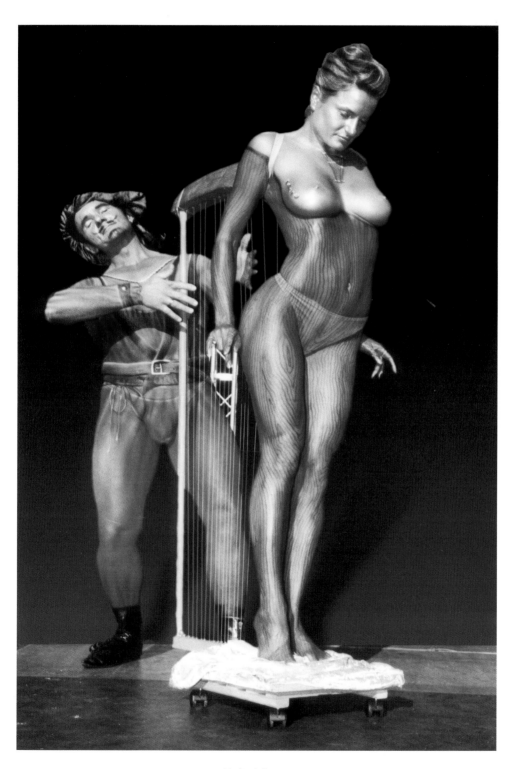

Norbert Bauer

Siegfried Brandstätter

Alois Endl

Wolf Reicherter

Wolf Reicherter

www.wolf-bodymagic.de

If the world of bodypainting is made up of day and night then the art of the dark hours has to be UV bodypainting. And if this world is made of kings and queens then the king of UV is Wolf Reicherter. UV bodypainting requires the ability to see things not in shadow and light like most artists, but in fluorescence and empty black space. Wolf Reicherter's vision of the world is unique, and his artistic creations reflect his curious vision.

'The aim of my work is to transform human beings into arrangements of light, modern avatars and deities and ghostly apparitions. In the grey before time, before people began to develop clothing, they painted their bodies with fats and earth. A shaman painted from head to foot was the intermediate between his people and the otherworld.'

Painting with fluorescent colours is a separate technique that is vastly different to traditional brush and sponge or airbrush painting. Wolf was one of the first artists to make a study of this technique and has been the leader in his field for over a decade. His performances and photographs have astounded viewers all over Europe on stages, at festivals and in magazines.

'Bodymagic builds bridges from the ancient past of body art into the here and now. With colour and lights only made possible by modern technology I am able to create magical art onto living bodies. Bodymagic is archaic body art in the dawn of the 21st century.'

Wolf designs his artworks with a combination of tribal designs and with robotic future visions in bold colours. In UV design, patterns are stronger than pictures and lines more important than blending colours. Wolf also experiments with special effects and interesting props, to further enhance his art. Photographing with UV light is an art form that takes practice and patience. Wolf also photographs all his own projects and is as talented a photographer as painter.

Wolf works with a range of talented dancers and acrobats, and on stage his creations of light and empty space move with a combination of grace and madness that can be frightening and intriguing.

After winning numerous awards in the bodypainting industry Wolf has moved into teaching UV effects and UV photography. He continues to push his own boundaries with his art and to inspire many artists learning the intricacies of UV.

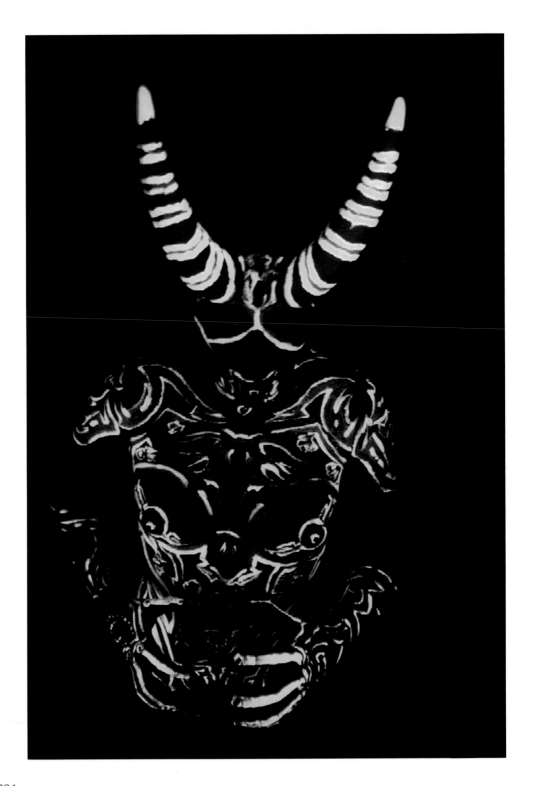

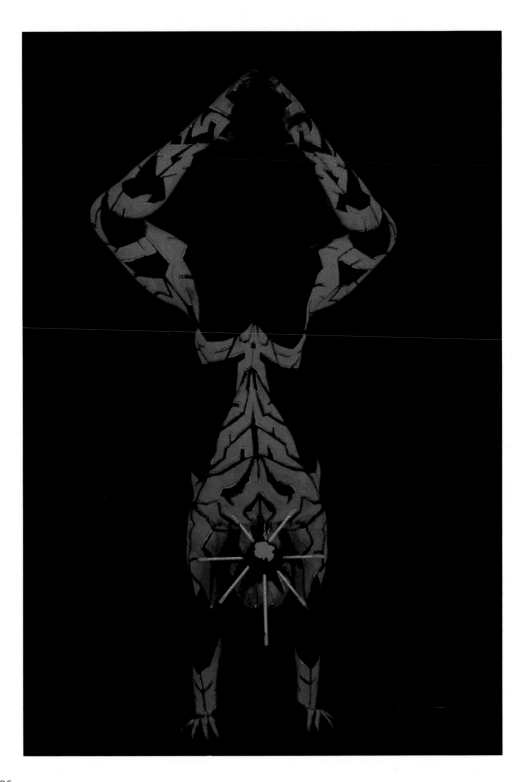

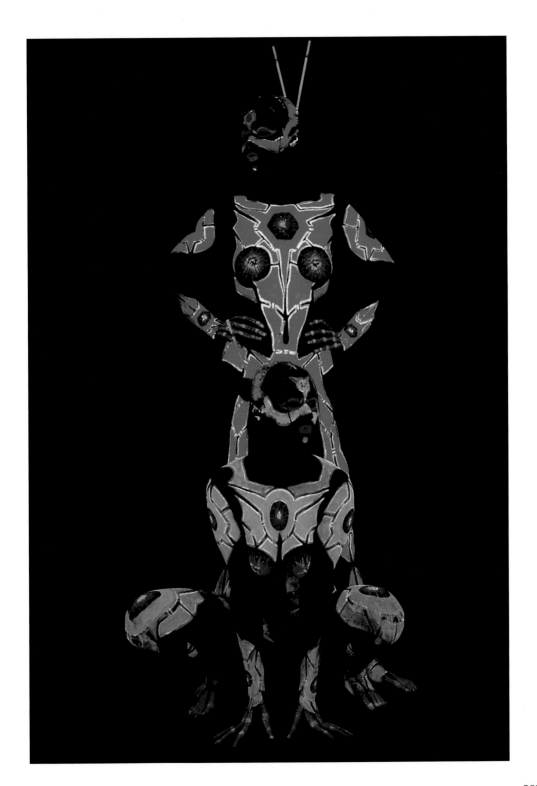

Printed in Austria by: Kreiner Druck 2008

Publisher: info@wbpa.info
World Body Painting Association   www.wbpa.info
World Bodypainting Festival   www.bodypainting-festival.com
Karala B   www.karala-b.com